# BIBLE TRIVIA QUIZ

500 QUESTIONS & ANSWERS!

CONOVER SWOFFORD

Previously released as *Can You Outsmart a Sunday Schooler?*



ISBN 978-1-63609-735-0



Published by Barbour Publishing, Inc., 1810 Barbour Drive, Uhrichsville, Ohio 44683, www.barbourbooks.com

*Our mission is to inspire the world with the life-changing message of the Bible.*

Printed in the United States of America.

# CONTENTS

# INTRODUCTION

So, how well did you listen during Sunday school and church? Find out with *Bible Trivia Quiz*!

This collection of 50 ten-question quizzes will test your knowledge of favorite Bible stories and topics, covering categories like:

- the Acts of the Apostles
- cities
- husbands and wives
- numbers
- parables
- the Word of God

Answers follow the tenth question of each quiz.

## Scoring

Answer *eight or more* in each quiz, and you outsmart the Sunday schoolers.

Answer *five to seven* questions, you're still in Sunday school.

Answer *four or fewer* correctly, you need to get to Sunday school. . .fast!

# YOUNG PEOPLE IN THE BIBLE

It doesn't matter to God how old you are. What matters is that you're willing to serve Him. Here are some young people in the Bible who God used in amazing ways. How much do you know about them?

### Question #1

Before Daniel was taken captive to Babylon, he was a:

a) prince
b) shepherd
c) musician
d) cupbearer

### Question #2

Moses' sister who watched over him in his basket in the river was:

a) Deborah
b) Ruth
c) Esther
d) Miriam

### Question #3

David was the youngest of how many brothers?

a) six
b) seven
c) eight
d) nine

## Question #4

The Hebrew maid who told her mistress that Elisha could cure leprosy served the wife of:

a) Jehu
b) Jehoram
c) Naaman
d) Nehemiah

## Question #5

Who was thrown into a pit and then sold into slavery by his own brothers?

a) Reuben
b) Simeon
c) Joseph
d) Benjamin

## Question #6

The youngest king of Judah was how old when he began to reign?

a) seven
b) eight
c) ten
d) twelve

## Question #7

The second-youngest king of Judah was how old when he began to reign?

a) eight
b) ten
c) twelve
d) fourteen

## Question #8

The boy who gave Jesus his lunch had:

a) two loaves and five fish
b) three loaves and five fish
c) five loaves and two fish
d) five loaves and three fish

## Question #9

When Samuel was dedicated to God's service, he worked for which priest?

a) Phinehas
b) Eli
c) Abimelech
d) Melchizedek

## Question #10

How old was Jarius' daughter when Jesus raised her from the dead?

a) 10
b) 12
c) 14
d) 16

# YOUNG PEOPLE IN THE BIBLE ANSWERS

1. a) prince (Daniel 1:3, 6)
2. d) Miriam (Exodus 2:3–4; Numbers 26:59)
3. c) eight (1 Samuel 16:10–11)
4. c) Naaman (2 Kings 5:1–3)
5. c) Joseph (Genesis 37:26–28)
6. a) seven (2 Kings 11:2–4, 12)
7. a) eight (2 Kings 22:1)
8. c) five loaves and two fish (John 6:9)
9. b) Eli (1 Samuel 1:20–25)
10. b) 12 (Luke 8:41–42, 54–55)

**So, how did you do?**

# BY ANY OTHER NAME

Sometimes we know a biblical character by one name, but the Bible also gives us another less familiar name for that person. Or we may know biblical characters by their names but not by their titles. How familiar are you with these lesser-known names and titles of famous biblical characters?

### Question #1

Esther's Hebrew name was:

a) Ruth
b) Deborah
c) Hadassah
d) Miriam

### Question #2

Belteshazzar was the Babylonian name for:

a) Jeremiah
b) Daniel
c) Ezekiel
d) Nehemiah

### Question #3

Hananiah's Babylonian name was:

a) Shadrach
b) Meshach
c) Abednego
d) Nebuchadnezzar

## Question #4

Which two disciples did Jesus call "the sons of thunder"?

a) Peter and Andrew
b) James and John
c) Peter and James
d) Andrew and John

## Question #5

Who was given Zaphnath-paaneah as his Egyptian name?

a) Moses
b) Jacob
c) Joseph
d) Benjamin

## Question #6

What man in the Bible is specifically referred to as "the Jews' enemy"?

a) Pharaoh
b) Herod
c) Haman
d Judas

## Question #7

What priest's sons were called "sons of Belial"?

a) Aaron
b) Eli
c) Samuel
d) Phinehas

## Question #8

Whom did Jesus say was the "son of perdition"?

a) Satan
b) Herod
c) Judas
d) Pilate

## Question #9

Of the seven chosen in Acts 6:5, which one was referred to as "the evangelist"?

a) Stephen
b) Philip
c) Nicolas
d) Timon

## Question #10

Whom did Jesus say was the greatest man ever born?

a) Moses
b) Abraham
c) Adam
d) John the Baptist

## BY ANY OTHER NAME ANSWERS

1. c) Hadassah (Esther 2:7)
2. b) Daniel (Daniel 1:7)
3. a) Shadrach (Daniel 1:7)
4. b) James and John (Mark 3:17)
5. c) Joseph (Genesis 41:45)
6. c) Haman (Esther 3:10)
7. b) Eli (1 Samuel 2:12)
8. c) Judas (John 17:12; 18:2)
9. b) Philip (Acts 21:8)
10. d) John the Baptist (Matthew 11:11)

**So, how did you do?**

# BIBLICAL DREAMS

Some people in the Bible had some very strange dreams. Sometimes the dream was a vision that needed interpretation. Sometimes God gave specific instructions to someone in a dream. What do you know about these people and their dreams?

## Question #1

Jacob dreamed of a ___________ that went to heaven.

a) staircase
b) ladder
c) mountain
d) chariot

## Question #2

Pharaoh dreamed that seven skinny ___________ ate seven fat ___________.

a) cattle
b) sheep
c) horses
d) fish

## Question #3

When Nebuchadnezzar dreamed of a strange figure, who interpreted his dream for him?

a) Babylonian wise men
b) Joseph
c) Daniel
d) astrologers

## Question #4

Where were Joseph, the butler, and the baker when Joseph interpreted dreams for them?

a) Pharaoh's palace
b) a field
c) jail
d) Joseph's house

## Question #5

Who dreamed that he was a sheaf of wheat and other sheaves bowed down to him?

a) Judah
b) Joseph
c) Daniel
d) Moses

## Question #6

Who saw a sheet full of creatures and was told to "rise and eat"?

a) John
b) Peter
c) Stephen
d) James

## Question #7

Who was warned in a dream not to go back to Herod?

a) wise men
b) shepherds
c) Joseph
d) John the Baptist

## Question #8

Who was told in a dream to take a wife, even though she was expecting a child?

a) Hosea
b) Joseph
c) Moses
d) Jacob

## Question #9

Who was disturbed because she had a dream about Jesus?

a) Mary Magdalene
b) Martha
c) Herodias
d) Pilate's wife

## Question #10

In Daniel's prophetic dream of kingdoms to come, how many beasts did Daniel see?

a) two
b) three
c) four
d) seven

## BIBLICAL DREAMS ANSWERS

1. b) ladder (Genesis 28:12)
2. a) cattle (Genesis 41:20)
3. c) Daniel (Daniel 2:24)
4. c) jail (Genesis 40:1–3)
5. b) Joseph (Genesis 37:5–7)
6. b) Peter (Acts 10:9–13)
7. a) wise men (Matthew 2:1, 12)
8. b) Joseph (Matthew 1:20)
9. d) Pilate's wife (Matthew 27:17–19)
10. c) four (Daniel 7:3)

**So, how did you do?**

# FOREIGN KINGS AND QUEENS

The Bible mentions many kings and queens who influenced the nation of Israel. Some were good and some were evil. What do you know about these other countries and their monarchs?

### Question #1

Balak, who hired Balaam to curse the Israelites, was king of the:

a) Moabites
b) Amorites
c) Hittites
d) Edomites

### Question #2

The queen who came to visit Solomon was from:

a) Babylon
b) Egypt
c) Sheba
d) Ethiopia

### Question #3

King Hiram (or Huram), from whom Solomon got materials to build the temple, was king of:

a) Tyre
b) Sidon
c) Zoar
d) Syria

## Question #4

Melchizedek was a priest, but he was also king of:

a) Jericho
b) Zion
c) Jerusalem
d) Salem

## Question #5

What was the official title of the Herod who ruled during Jesus and John the Baptist's ministry?

a) king
b) prince
c) tetrarch
d) governor

## Question #6

The king of Babylon who took the southern kingdom of Judah captive was:

a) Darius
b) Nebuchadnezzar
c) Cyrus
d) Belshazzar

## Question #7

The king of what country took the northern kingdom of Israel captive?

a) Egypt
b) Assyria
c) Syria
d) Samaria

## Question #8

The name of the king who allowed the Israelites to return to Jerusalem from their captivity in Babylon was:

a) Nebuchadnezzar
b) Darius
c) Cyrus
d) Xerxes

## Question #9

The king who saw the handwriting on the wall was:

a) Belshazzar
b) Nebuchadnezzar
c) Darius
d) Cyrus

## Question #10

The name of the queen who ruled before Esther was:

a) Bathsheba
b) Vashti
c) Abigail
d) Ahinoam

# FOREIGN KINGS AND QUEENS
## ANSWERS

1. a) Moabites (Numbers 22:1–6)
2. c) Sheba (2 Chronicles 9:1)
3. a) Tyre (2 Chronicles 2:3)
4. d) Salem (Genesis 14:18)
5. c) tetrarch (Luke 3:1)
6. b) Nebuchadnezzar (2 Chronicles 36:6)
7. b) Assyria (2 Kings 17:6)
8. c) Cyrus (Ezra 1:1–2)
9. a) Belshazzar (Daniel 5:1–5)
10. b) Vashti (Esther 1:9)

**So, how did you do?**

# GOD'S WARRIORS

The night before the battle of Jericho, Joshua asked the captain of the Lord's host, "Art thou for us, or for our adversaries?" (Joshua 5:13). That's the question God asks His people: "Are you for Me or for My adversaries?" Who is on the Lord's side? The warriors in this quiz were. What do you know about them?

## Question #1

To which of His warriors did God say, "Have not I commanded thee? Be strong and of a good courage"?

a) Moses
b) David
c) Joshua
d) Jacob

## Question #2

What woman nailed an enemy general's head to the ground?

a) Jael
b) Deborah
c) Esther
d) Miriam

## Question #3

What Jewish leader rebuilt the wall of Jerusalem with a sword strapped to his side?

a) David
b) Solomon
c) Nehemiah
d) Hezekiah

## Question #4

Whose army fought with pitchers and lamps and shouted, "The sword of the LORD, and of ____________"?

a) Saul
b) Gideon
c) David
d) Joshua

## Question #5

King Saul's warrior son who was David's friend was:

a) Ish-bosheth
b) Ishvi
c) Malchi-shua
d) Jonathan

## Question #6

Which of God's prophets called down fire on two separate cohorts of fifty men each who had been sent to capture him?

a) Elijah
b) Elisha
c) Jeremiah
d) Isaiah

## Question #7

Which judge of Israel who fought the Ammonites was described as "a mighty man of valour"?

a) Abimelech
b) Jephthah
c) Tola
d) Jair

## Question #8

Because Moses claimed he was slow of speech, whom did God send with him to confront Pharaoh?

a) Joshua
b) Caleb
c) Aaron
d) Amram

## Question #9

Who was told, "Who knoweth whether thou art come to the kingdom for such a time as this?"—meaning that she might save her people.

a) Deborah
b) Miriam
c) Esther
d) Ruth

## Question #10

Whom did God appoint to wipe out Ahab, Jezebel, and their evil offspring?

a) Elijah
b) Elisha
c) Jehu
d) Isaiah

## GOD'S WARRIORS ANSWERS

1. c) Joshua (Joshua 1:9)
2. a) Jael (Judges 4:21)
3. c) Nehemiah (Nehemiah 4:18)
4. b) Gideon (Judges 7:18)
5. d) Jonathan (1 Samuel 19:2)
6. a) Elijah (2 Kings 1:10–14)
7. b) Jephthah (Judges 11:1)
8. c) Aaron (Exodus 4:10–16)
9. c) Esther (Esther 4:13–14)
10. c) Jehu (2 Kings 9:1–8)

**So, how did you do?**

# PROPHETS

Hebrews 1:1 says that in the old days God spoke in diverse ways to the fathers by the prophets. The prophets prophesied good things and bad things and reported all the things God told them to. Sometimes they were listened to; sometimes they were persecuted. Do you know these prophets?

## Question #1

What prophet did God hide by the brook Cherith and command ravens to feed?

a) Isaiah
b) Jeremiah
c) Elijah
d) Elisha

## Question #2

What was the test to see if a prophet was speaking God's word or not?

a) his face would shine
b) his words would be eloquent
c) what he said would come to pass
d) all of the above

## Question #3

Deuteronomy 18:17–18 says that a prophet would be raised up like:

a) Abraham
b) Moses
c) Joseph
d) Elijah

## Question #4

What Old Testament prophet saw the Lord sitting on a throne?

a) Elijah
b) Elisha
c) Isaiah
d) Daniel

## Question #5

What prophet was taken to heaven in a whirlwind and a chariot of fire?

a) Moses
b) Isaiah
c) Elijah
d) Elisha

## Question #6

Who was known as the "runaway prophet"?

a) Jeremiah
b) Joel
c) Jonah
d) Jehu

## Question #7

What two prophets appeared to Jesus on the Mount of Transfiguration?

a) Elijah and Elisha
b) Isaiah and Jeremiah
c) Moses and Elisha
d) Moses and Elijah

## Question #8

What king had a proverb written about him that said, "Is ____________ also among the prophets?"

a) Saul
b) David
c) Solomon
d) Hezekiah

## Question #9

What two prophets who also wrote books of the Bible are mentioned together in the book of Ezra?

a) Haggai and Zechariah
b) Habakkuk and Zephaniah
c) Micah and Amos
d) Isaiah and Jeremiah

## Question #10

Who did God say that He had ordained to be a prophet before he was born?

a) Isaiah
b) Micah
c) Amos
d) Jeremiah

## PROPHETS ANSWERS

1. c) Elijah (1 Kings 17:1–4)
2. c) what he said would come to pass (Deuteronomy 18:22)
3. b) Moses
4. c) Isaiah (Isaiah 6:1)
5. c) Elijah (2 Kings 2:11)
6. c) Jonah (Jonah 1:3)
7. d) Moses and Elijah (or Elias) (Matthew 17:3)
8. a) Saul (1 Samuel 10:12)
9. a) Haggai and Zechariah (Ezra 5:1)
10. d) Jeremiah (Jeremiah 1:5)

**So, how did you do?**

# THE B-I-B-L-E

The Bible is the Word of God. How much do you know about its various properties? Who wrote it? How long is it? With which of the following facts are you familiar?

### Question #1

How many chapters are in the Song of Solomon?

a) four
b) six
c) eight
d) ten

### Question #2

What book of the New Testament is totally dedicated to describing God's love for us?

a) 1 John
b) 2 Peter
c) Romans
d) 1 Corinthians

### Question #3

What is the longest chapter in the Bible?

a) Psalm 19
b) Psalm 119
c) Revelation 20
d) 1 Corinthians 15

## Question #4

What two books of the Bible mention the tree of life?

a) Genesis and Psalms
b) Genesis and Proverbs
c) Genesis and Revelation
d) Genesis and Matthew

## Question #5

How many books are in the Old Testament?

a) twenty-seven
b) twenty-nine
c) thirty-seven
d) thirty-nine

## Question #6

How many books are in the New Testament?

a) twenty-seven
b) twenty-nine
c) thirty-seven
d) thirty-nine

## Question #7

What is the last book of the Old Testament?

a) Haggai
b) Zephaniah
c) Zechariah
d) Malachi

## Question #8

The first five books of the Bible are commonly referred to as the books of:

a) law
b) history
c) poetry
d) prophecy

## Question #9

How many books of the Bible start with the letter *J*?

a) eight
b) ten
c) twelve
d) fourteen

## Question #10

How many books of the Bible have only one chapter?

a) two
b) three
c) four
d) five

1. c) eight
2. a) 1 John
3. b) Psalm 119
4. c) Genesis and Revelation
   (Genesis 3:22; Revelation 2:7)
5. d) thirty-nine
6. a) twenty-seven
7. d) Malachi
8. a) law
9. c) twelve (Joshua, Judges, Job, Jeremiah, Joel, Jonah, John, James, 1 John, 2 John, 3 John, Jude)
10. d) five (Obadiah, Philemon, 2 John, 3 John, Jude)

**So, how did you do?**

# GOD'S QUESTIONS

Many times when God spoke to His people, He asked them questions. Sometimes He spoke to them directly and sometimes He spoke to them through a prophet or an angel. Do you know to whom God was speaking when He asked the following questions?

### Question #1

"Why art thou wroth [angry]?"

a) Elijah
b) Abraham
c) Cain
d) Adam

### Question #2

"What is that in thine hand?"

a) David
b) Moses
c) Saul
d) Jacob

### Question #3

"Ask what I shall give thee."

a) Solomon
b) David
c) Abraham
d) Isaac

## Question #4

"Whence comest thou?"

a) Paul
b) Satan
c) Esau
d) Noah

## Question #5

"Where wast thou when I laid the foundations of the earth?"

a) Adam
b) Noah
c) Job
d) Elijah

## Question #6

"Whom shall I send, and who will go for us?"

a) Isaiah
b) Ezekiel
c) Daniel
d) Jeremiah

## Question #7

"Doest thou well to be angry?"

a) Job
b) Jeremiah
c) Jonah
d) James

## Question #8

"Is any thing too hard for the Lord?"

a) Abraham
b) Isaac
c) Jacob
d) Joseph

## Question #9

"What have I done unto thee? and wherein have I wearied thee?"

a) Solomon
b) Jeremiah
c) the nation of Israel
d) Pharaoh

## Question #10

"Where art thou?"

a) Adam
b) Eve
c) Adam and Eve
d) the serpent

# GOD'S QUESTIONS
## ANSWERS

1. c) Cain (Genesis 4:6)
2. b) Moses (Exodus 4:1–2)
3. a) Solomon (1 Kings 3:5)
4. b) Satan (Job 1:7)
5. c) Job (Job 38:4)
6. a) Isaiah (Isaiah 6:8)
7. c) Jonah (Jonah 4:4)
8. a) Abraham (Genesis 18:14)
9. c) the nation of Israel (Micah 6:3)
10. a) Adam (Genesis 3:9)

**So, how did you do?**

# JUDGES

The book of Judges shows how the Israelites followed a destructive cycle. Things would be going well, and the Israelites would start following other gods. Then they would be oppressed by some enemy and cry out to the Lord. The Lord would raise up a judge to deliver them. After they were delivered, the Israelites would remain faithful to the Lord as long as the judge lived. When the judge died, the Israelites would once again start worshipping other gods. The book of Judges shows the faithfulness of God to deliver His people. What do you know about these judges?

## Question #1

What judge turned down the opportunity to be king when the people of Israel offered him that position?

a) Abdon
b) Tola
c) Gideon
d) Jair

## Question #2

Who was the judge set apart to God by a Nazarite vow?

a) Othniel
b) Samson
c) Jephthah
d) Gideon

## Question #3

What was the judge Othniel's relationship to the good spy Caleb?

a) nephew to uncle
b) brothers
c) son-in-law to father-in-law
d) both a and c

## Question #4

One judge had to fight the king of Moab named Eglon, who was described as:

a) a mighty warrior
b) a fierce warrior
c) a very fat man
d) an evil king

## Question #5

Who is known as the lefthanded judge?

a) Tola
b) Jair
c) Ehud
d) Othniel

## Question #6

Samson lost his strength when Delilah:

a) tied him to the bed
b) bound him with new ropes
c) wove his hair into a loom
d) cut his hair

## Question #7

The only female judge, Deborah, helped Barak fight against a general named:

a) Hazael
b) Jehu
c) Sisera
d) Anak

## Question #8

The enemies whom Samson fought were the:

a) Moabites
b) Ammonites
c) Canaanites
d) Philistines

## Question #9

Jephthah vowed to sacrifice the first thing that came out of his house if he won the battle against the Ammonites. What came out of his house?

a) a cow
b) a sheep
c) a dog
d) his daughter

## Question #10

What kind of tree did the judge Deborah live under?

a) sycamore
b) fig
c) palm
d) tamarisk

# JUDGES ANSWERS

1. c) Gideon (Judges 8:22–23)
2. b) Samson (Judges 13:5, 24)
3. d) both a and c (Judges 1:13)
4. c) a very fat man (Judges 3:17)
5. c) Ehud (Judges 3:15)
6. d) cut his hair (Judges 16:19–20)
7. c) Sisera (Judges 4:13–14)
8. d) Philistines (Judges 16:30)
9. d) his daughter (Judges 11:30–34)
10. c) palm (Judges 4:4–5)

**So, how did you do?**

# KINGS OF JUDAH

Unlike the kings of Israel, who were all evil, there were some good kings of Judah—as well as some stinkers. The kings of Judah were all descended from David, and it was from this kingly line that Jesus came. Which of these kings do you know?

### Question #1

Who was king when the kingdom split into ten northern tribes (Israel) and two southern tribes (Judah)?

a) Solomon
b) Rehoboam
c) Hezekiah
d) David

### Question #2

What wicked king reigned fifty-five years after being crowned at age twelve?

a) Asa
b) Manasseh
c) Jeconiah
d) Jehoram

### Question #3

What king of Judah nearly died in his thirties, but got fifteen additional years of life after praying?

a) Ahaz
b) Jotham
c) Ahaz
d) Hezekiah

## Question #4

What king of Judah went into battle in support of his counterpart from Israel and narrowly escaped death?

a) Jehoshaphat
b) Uzziah
c) Manasseh
d) Jehoahaz

## Question #5

What king's grandmother tried to kill all of her grandchildren so she could be queen?

a) Joash
b) Hezekiah
c) Manasseh
d) Josiah

## Question #6

About what boy king does the Bible say there was none before him or after him "that turned to the Lord with all his heart"?

a) Joash
b) Jehoram
c) Jehu
d) Josiah

## Question #7

Uzziah was one of the really good kings of Judah, but God struck him with leprosy because he:

a) accidentally killed someone
b) took God's name in vain
c) burned incense in the temple
d) b and c

## Question #8

What wicked king was killed by his own officials after ruling only two years?

a) Abijah
b) Amon
c) Jehoahaz
d) Ahaziah

## Question #9

How old was Joash when he became king of Judah?

a) seven
b) seventeen
c) twenty-seven
d) forty-seven

## Question #10

Who was king when the kingdom of Judah was taken into Babylonian captivity?

a) Hezekiah
b) Manasseh
c) Jehoiakim
d) Hazael

# KINGS OF JUDAH ANSWERS

1. b) Rehoboam (1 Kings 12:19–21)
2. b) Manasseh (2 Kings 21:1–3)
3. d) Hezekiah (2 Kings 20:1–6)
4. a) Jehoshaphat (1 Kings 22:1–4, 32–33)
5. a) Joash (2 Chronicles 22:10–11)
6. d) Josiah (2 Kings 23:24–25)
7. c) burned incense in the temple (2 Chronicles 26:19–20)
8. b) Amon (2 Kings 21:19–23)
9. a) seven (2 Kings 11:1–12)
10. c) Jehoiakim (2 Chronicles 36:5–6)

**So, how did you do?**

# RULERS OF ISRAEL

After the kingdom split into Israel and Judah, there was not one king of Israel whom the Bible refers to as good. Nor was there a royal succession. The kings of Israel usually became king by killing a predecessor. What do you know about these bad boys (and girl)?

## Question #1

What was the shortest reign of a king of Israel?

a) one day
b) seven days
c) three weeks
d) two months

## Question #2

After the kingdom split into ten northern tribes (Israel) and two southern tribes (Judah), who was the first king of those northern tribes?

a) Jehu
b) Ahab
c) Jeroboam
d) Jotham

## Question #3

Which king does the Bible say "did evil in the sight of the LORD above all that were before him"?

a) Ahab
b) Zimri
c) Omri
d) Tibni

## Question #4

Whom did Queen Jezebel have stoned to death so her husband, Ahab, could steal his vineyard?

a) Nehemiah
b) Nabal
c) Naboth
d) Nathan

## Question #5

What army commander was appointed by God to be king of Israel, with a command to destroy the remainder of the evil Ahab's family?

a) Nadab
b) Elah
c) Baasha
d) Jehu

## Question #6

What nation took the ten northern tribes into captivity?

a) Assyria
b) Syria
c) Babylon
d) Egypt

## Question #7

Who was king when the ten northern tribes were taken into captivity?

a) Ahab
b) Zimri
c) Hoshea
d) Omni

## Question #8

What sinful objects did Israel's first king set up in the towns of Bethel and Dan?

a) statues of himself
b) golden calves
c) Asherah poles
d) temples to the sun

## Question #9

What was the longest reign of a king in the northern nation of Israel?

a) fifteen years
b) twenty-one years
c) forty-one years
d) sixty years

## Question #10

After the kingdom split, how many kings did the ten northern tribes have before they were taken into captivity?

a) six
b) twelve
c) twenty
d) forty-nine

# RULERS OF ISRAEL
## ANSWERS

1. b) seven days (1 Kings 16:15)
2. c) Jeroboam (1 Kings 11:31)
3. a) Ahab (1 Kings 16:30)
4. c) Naboth (1 Kings 21:8–11)
5. d) Jehu (1 Kings 19:15–17)
6. a) Assyria (2 Kings 17:6)
7. c) Hoshea (2 Kings 17:6)
8. b) golden calves (1 Kings 12:26–29)
9. c) forty-one years (2 Kings 14:23)
10. c) twenty (Jeroboam I, Nadab, Baasha, Elah, Zimri, Tibni, Omri, Ahab, Ahaziah, Joram, Jehu, Jehoahaz, Joah, Jeroboam II, Zechariah, Shallum, Menahem, Pekahiah, Pekah, Hoshea)

**So, how did you do?**

# FALSE GODS

All through the Old Testament, God's people turned from worshipping Him and instead worshipped false gods and idols. It broke God's heart and caused all kinds of troubles for the Israelites. Some of the false gods are more well known to us than others. How many have you heard of?

### Question #1

What golden idol did Moses' brother, Aaron, create for the people when Moses stayed long with God on Mount Sinai?

a) a snake
b) an eagle
c) a frog
d) a calf

### Question #2

What was the name of the princess of Sidon (or Zidon) who introduced Baal worship to Israel?

a) Bathsheba
b) Athaliah
c) Jezebel
d) Abigail

## Question #3

What popular idol did Hezekiah, king of Judah, destroy?

a) the brass snake Moses made in the wilderness
b) the golden calf Aaron had crafted
c) the "queen of heaven"
d) Ashteroth

## Question #4

What was the name of the Philistine idol that fell facedown in front of the ark of the covenant?

a) Molech
b) Chemosh
c) Beelzebub
d) Dagon

## Question #5

Into what did the good king of Judah, Josiah, transform places of idolatry?

a) cemeteries
b) sewers
c) wastelands
d) potters' fields

## Question #6

In what city was the New Testament idol to the goddess Diana?

a) Philippi
b) Macedonia
c) Ephesus
d) Colosse

## Question #7

What prophet saw twenty-five men worshipping the sun with their backs to God's temple?

a) Hosea
b) Ezekiel
c) Micah
d) Malachi

## Question #8

What king of God's people was the first to build places for the worship of Chemosh and Molech?

a) Ahab
b) Jehu
c) Solomon
d) Zimri

## Question #9

What judge of Israel pulled down his own father's altar to Baal because God commanded him to?

a) Samson
b) Othniel
c) Gideon
d) Jephthah

## Question #10

What king had Daniel thrown in the lions' den because Daniel refused to pray to him instead of to God?

a) Nebuchadnezzar
b) Darius
c) Cyrus
d) Belshazzar

1. d) a calf (Exodus 32:1–4)
2. c) Jezebel (1 Kings 16:31–32)
3. a) the brass snake Moses made in the wilderness (2 Kings 18:1, 4)
4. d) Dagon (1 Samuel 5:1–3)
5. a) cemeteries (2 Kings 23:13–14)
6. c) Ephesus (Acts 19:24–28)
7. b) Ezekiel (Ezekiel 8:16)
8. c) Solomon (1 Kings 11:7)
9. c) Gideon (Judges 6:24–25)
10. b) Darius (Daniel 6:9–16)

**So, how did you do?**

# BAD GUYS AND GALS

All through the Bible there are stories of people who wanted their own way and would do anything to get it. They didn't care about God's will, just their own. These people are a warning to us about how *not* to behave. How well do you know their stories?

## Question #1

Who said to God, "My punishment is greater than I can bear"?

a) Ahab
b) Jezebel
c) Cain
d) Saul

## Question #2

Which queen "destroyed all the seed royal of the house of Judah" and took the throne for herself?

a) Bathsheba
b) Athaliah
c) Vashti
d) Jezebel

## Question #3

Nadab and Abihu, who were burned to death because they offered "strange fire" to the Lord, were the sons of what high priest?

a) Aaron
b) Caiaphas
c) Eli
d) Melchizedek

## Question #4

What prophet did Judah's King Zedekiah allow to be thrown into a muddy well?

a) Daniel
b) Joel
c) Zephaniah
d) Jeremiah

## Question #5

After Jacob worked seven years to earn the right to marry Rachel, who tricked him and gave him Leah instead?

a) Bethuel
b) Haran
c) Laban
d) Lot

## Question #6

Haman was so determined to kill Mordecai that he:

a) tried to kill all the Jews
b) built a gallows to hang Mordecai on
c) tried to stab Mordecai
d) both a and b

## Question #7

What group did Jesus most often target with His statement, "Woe unto you"?

a) tax collectors
b) scribes and Pharisees
c) prostitutes
d) Roman officials

## Question #8

Whom did Pharaoh tell to kill all the Hebrew baby boys?

a) midwives
b) soldiers
c) the babies' parents
d) his chief servant

## Question #9

Absalom, King David's son who led a rebellion against his father, was finally captured and killed because:

a) his hair got caught in a tree
b) his servants turned on him
c) the Lord struck him down
d) his own soldiers captured him

## Question #10

Who ordered John the Baptist's head to be cut off?

a) Herodias
b) Herod
c) Salome
d) Pilate

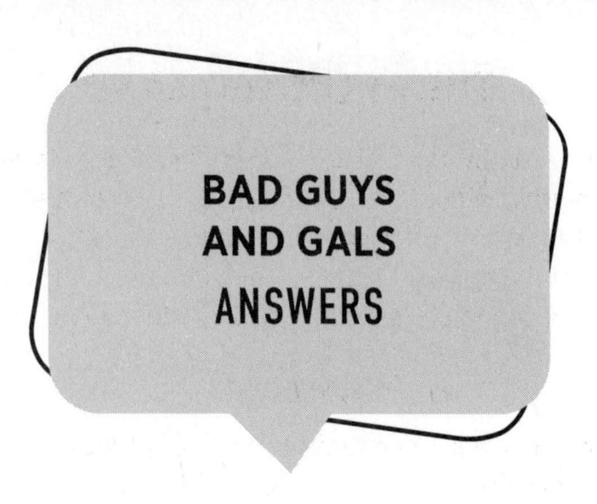


1. c) Cain (Genesis 4:13)
2. b) Athaliah (2 Chronicles 22:10, 12)
3. a) Aaron (Leviticus 10:1–2)
4. d) Jeremiah (Jeremiah 38:5–6)
5. c) Laban (Genesis 29:21–25)
6. d) both a and b (Esther 3:5–6; 5:14)
7. b) scribes and Pharisees (see, for example, Matthew 23:13, 14, 15, 23, 25)
8. a) midwives (Exodus 1:15–16)
9. a) his hair got caught in a tree (2 Samuel 14:25–26; 18:9)
10. b) Herod (Matthew 14:6–10)

**So, how did you do?**

# THE GARDEN OF EDEN

The garden of Eden was truly paradise on earth. God created this perfect garden so that human-kind would have a place to live and grow and learn about Him. How much have you learned about the garden of Eden and what happened there?

### Question #1

How many rivers were in Eden?

a) one
b) two
c) three
d) four

### Question #2

God made Eve from:

a) dust
b) clay
c) Adam's rib
d) fruit from the tree of knowledge

### Question #3

Which tree in the garden did the Lord command Adam *not* to eat from?

a) the tree of life
b) the tree of wisdom
c) the tree of evil
d) the tree of the knowledge of good and evil

## Question #4

What did God say would happen if Adam ate from the forbidden tree?

a) he would be banished
b) he would become sick
c) he would die
d) he would lose Eve

## Question #5

What did the serpent tell Eve would happen if she ate from the forbidden tree?

a) you will not die
b) you will become as gods
c) you will know good and evil
d) all of the above

## Question #6

After they ate from the forbidden tree, what was Adam and Eve's first reaction?

a) they got sick
b) they hid themselves
c) they clothed themselves
d) they ran away from the serpent

## Question #7

As a result of Adam's sin, God cursed:

a) Adam
b) the serpent
c) the ground
d) both b and c

## Question #8

According to God, when would Eve (and all women after her) find sorrow multiplied?

a) in childbirth
b) doing household duties
c) during sickness
d) in the night hours

## Question #9

God banished Adam and Eve from the garden to prevent them from:

a) hiding from Him
b) killing the serpent
c) living forever
d) destroying the forbidden tree

## Question #10

What did God send Adam out of the garden to do?

a) wander forever
b) hunt animals
c) build a city
d) till the ground

# THE GARDEN OF EDEN
## ANSWERS

1. a) one (Genesis 2:10)
2. c) Adam's rib (Genesis 2:21–22; 3:20)
3. d) the tree of the knowledge of good and evil (Genesis 2:16–17)
4. c) he would die (Genesis 2:16–17)
5. d) all of the above (Genesis 3:4–5)
6. c) they clothed themselves (Genesis 3:7)
7. d) both b and c (Genesis 3:14, 17)
8. a) in childbirth (Genesis 3:16)
9. c) living forever (Genesis 3:22)
10. d) till the ground (Genesis 3:23)

**So, how did you do?**

# WHERE IS THIS VERSE FOUND?

Sometimes we may quote a verse that is very familiar to us, but perhaps we're not so certain where to find it in the Bible. Following are ten well-known verses. Do you know their correct biblical references?

## Question #1

"Jesus wept."

a) Matthew 11:35
b) Mark 11:35
c) John 11:35
d) Luke 11:35

## Question #2

"Am I my brother's keeper?"

a) Genesis 2:9
b) Genesis 3:9
c) Genesis 4:9
d) Genesis 5:9

## Question #3

"Father, forgive them; for they know not what they do."

a) Luke 23:34
b) Matthew 23:34
c) John 19:34
d) Mark 14:34

## Question #4

"The Lord is my shepherd; I shall not want."

a) Psalm 1:1
b) Psalm 100:1
c) Psalm 23:1
d) Psalm 19:1

## Question #5

"For God so loved the world, that he gave his only begotten Son, that whosoever believeth in him should not perish, but have everlasting life."

a) John 1:16
b) John 2:16
c) John 3:16
d) John 4:16

## Question #6

"Make a joyful noise unto the Lord, all ye lands."

a) Psalm 1:1
b) Psalm 34:1
c) Psalm 90:1
d) Psalm 100:1

## Question #7

"With God all things are possible."

a) Matthew 19:26
b) Matthew 9:26
c) Matthew 11:26
d) Matthew 13:26

## Question #8

"Not my will, but thine, be done."

a) Luke 22:42
b) Matthew 26:39
c) Mark 14:36
d) all of the above

## Question #9

"Pride goeth before destruction, and an haughty spirit before a fall."

a) Proverbs 3:5
b) Proverbs 16:18
c) Proverbs 1:7
d) Proverbs 31:1

## Question #10

"Train up a child in the way he should go: and when he is old, he will not depart from it."

a) Proverbs 22:6
b) Ecclesiastes 3:3
c) Psalm 22:6
d) Proverbs 18:24

## WHERE IS THIS VERSE FOUND?
## ANSWERS

1. c) John 11:35
2. c) Genesis 4:9
3. a) Luke 23:34
4. c) Psalm 23:1
5. c) John 3:16
6. d) Psalm 100:1
7. a) Matthew 19:26
8. a) Luke 22:42
9. b) Proverbs 16:18
10. a) Proverbs 22:6

**So, how did you do?**

# TRIBES OF ISRAEL

The Israelites were proud of their heritage, and they kept lengthy records of their lineage in order to prove who they were and from whom they were descended. In addition to the following quiz, here is one more question: Can you name the twelve tribes of Israel?

### Question #1

The tribes were named for the twelve sons of:

a) Joseph
b) Jacob
c) Moses
d) Isaac

### Question #2

There are three Sauls mentioned in the Bible, two of major importance—King Saul and the man who became the apostle Paul. They were both from the tribe of:

a) Levi
b) Ephraim
c) Judah
d) Benjamin

## Question #3

Joseph was forefather of which two tribes?

a) Manasseh and Ephraim
b) Gad and Dan
c) Manasseh and Naphtali
d) Ephraim and Dan

## Question #4

From what tribe was John the Baptist?

a) Judah
b) Reuben
c) Levi
d) Benjamin

## Question #5

How many women gave birth to the forefathers of the twelve tribes of Israel?

a) one
b) two
c) four
d) twelve

## Question #6

Forty-two thousand men of Ephraim were slaughtered because they could not pronounce the word:

a) *maranatha*
b) *anathema*
c) *shibboleth*
d) *hosanna*

## Question #7

When Israel entered the promised land, parts of how many tribes stayed east of Jordan?

a) three
b) six
c) nine
d) twelve

## Question #8

When the kingdom of Israel split into the northern ten tribes and the southern two tribes, which tribe aligned with Judah in the south?

a) Reuben
b) Naphtali
c) Benjamin
d) Levi

## Question #9

Which of these Z names is a tribe of Israel?

a) Zechariah
b) Zephaniah
c) Zipporah
d) Zebulun

## Question #10

In the lists of the tribes of Israel, which tribe is almost always listed first?

a) Judah
b) Reuben
c) Simeon
d) Levi

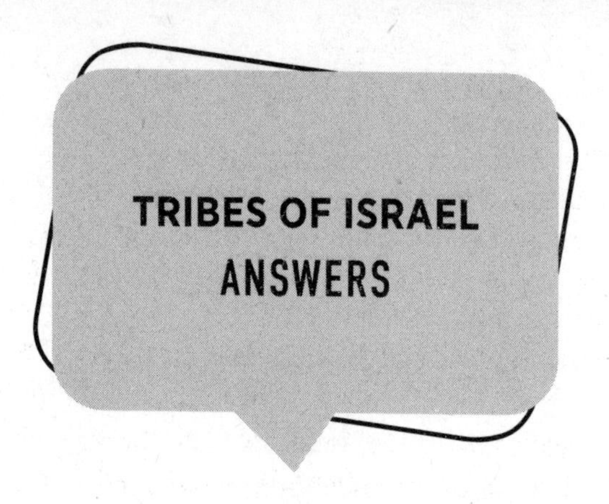


1. b) Jacob (Exodus 1:1–6)
2. d) Benjamin (1 Samuel 9:1–2; Philippians 3:5)
3. a) Manasseh and Ephraim (Genesis 48:1–6)
4. c) Levi, because his father was a priest (Deuteronomy 21:5; Luke 1:5–13, 57–60)
5. c) four (Genesis 35:22–26)
6. c) *shibboleth* (Judges 12:5–6)
7. a) three (Numbers 32:31–33)
8. c) Benjamin (1 Kings 12:23)
9. d) Zebulun (Genesis 49:13)
10. b) Reuben (Genesis 49:1–3)

**So, how did you do?**

# GOD'S LITTLE THINGS

The Bible says that God uses foolish things to confound the wise, and He uses weak things to confound the mighty. Nothing is too small for God to use to His glory. Of course, we have to be willing to let Him use us. What do you know about these little things God used?

### Question #1

Because Rahab believed in God and hid the Israelite spies, God told her she would not perish in Jericho if she bound a ___________ in her window.

a) new rope
b) leather belt
c) golden chain
d) scarlet thread

### Question #2

How many stones did David take out of the brook when he went to fight Goliath?

a) one
b) three
c) five
d) twelve

### Question #3

Shamgar was a judge of Israel who used what to slay six hundred Philistines?

a) an ox goad
b) a broken sword
c) a sling
d) a shepherd's staff

## Question #4

To prove His choice for high priest, God made Aaron's rod:

a) longer
b) shorter
c) turn into a snake
d) blossom

## Question #5

What did Samson use to slay a thousand of Israel's enemies?

a) an ox goad
b) the jawbone of an ass
c) a millstone
d) firebrands

## Question #6

When a prophet's widow needed money to save her sons, Elisha multiplied her last pot of:

a) oil
b) corn
c) meal
d) wine

## Question #7

When Jesus needed to pay the temple tax, where did He direct Peter to find a coin?

a) in a nearby field
b) in the mouth of a fish
c) in the middle of the road
d) in a hole in a tree

## Question #8

When the poor widow gave her two mites, she gave:

a) what the temple required
b) money that she had found
c) everything she had
d) what the priest told her to give

## Question #9

When Moses asked the people to bring offerings for the making of the tabernacle, they brought gold:

a) bracelets
b) earrings
c) rings
d) all of the above

## Question #10

When Elisha succeeded Elijah, what did the new prophet receive from the old prophet as a symbol?

a) a mantle
b) a rod
c) a ring
d) a robe

# GOD'S LITTLE THINGS ANSWERS

1. d) scarlet thread (Joshua 2:18)
2. c) five (1 Samuel 17:40)
3. a) an ox goad (Judges 3:31)
4. d) blossom (Numbers 17:1–8)
5. b) the jawbone of an ass (Judges 15:16)
6. a) oil (2 Kings 4:1–7)
7. b) in the mouth of a fish (Matthew 17:24–27)
8. c) everything she had (Mark 12:42–44)
9. d) all of the above (Exodus 35:5, 21–22)
10. a) a mantle (2 Kings 2:9–13)

**So, how did you do?**

# BIBLICAL RELATIVES

The Bible is full of families. Just like today's families, some are well-functioning and some are dysfunctional. All of them are there for us to learn from. Family lineage was extremely important in the Bible. It's interesting to see who was related to whom and how. What do you know about the following families?

## Question #1

Mephibosheth was the son of:

a) David
b) Saul
c) Jonathan
d) Jesse

## Question #2

David was Solomon's father—but who was Solomon's mother?

a) Michal
b) Abigail
c) Bathsheba
d) Abishag

## Question #3

What was Methuselah's relationship to Noah?

a) father
b) grandfather
c) great-grandfather
d) great-great-grandfather

## Question #4

How were Ruth and Boaz related to David?

a) grandparents
b) aunt and uncle
c) cousins
d) great-grandparents

## Question #5

How was Jesus related to John the Baptist?

a) their mothers were cousins
b) their fathers were cousins
c) Jesus' mother and John's father were cousins
d) Jesus' earthly father and John's mother were cousins

## Question #6

Lot was Abraham's:

a) nephew
b) cousin
c) uncle
d) brother

## Question #7

How was Seth related to Cain?

a) son
b) brother
c) nephew
d) uncle

## Question #8

Jochebed was Moses':

a) mother
b) mother-in-law
c) father
d) father-in-law

## Question #9

Jesus' disciples James and John were:

a) cousins
b) brothers
c) father and son
d) uncle and nephew

## Question #10

Samuel's mother, who prayed to have a son and then dedicated him to God, was:

a) Hannah
b) Ruth
c) Rachel
d) Leah

1. c) Jonathan (2 Samuel 9:6)
2. c) Bathsheba (1 Kings 1:11)
3. b) grandfather (Genesis 5:25–29)
4. d) great-grandparents (Ruth 4:21–22)
5. a) their mothers were cousins (Luke 1:36, 60)
6. a) nephew (Genesis 11:31)
7. b) brother (Genesis 4:1; 5:3)
8. a) mother (Exodus 6:20)
9. b) brothers (Matthew 4:21)
10. a) Hannah (1 Samuel 1:9–11, 19–20)

**So, how did you do?**

# HUMBLING EXPERIENCES

"Wherefore let him that thinketh he standeth take heed lest he fall" (1 Corinthians 10:12). Sometimes it is when we feel strongest that we make mistakes. Mistakes can be a good learning tool if we only look at them in the right light. The following biblical situations have a lot to teach us. What do you already know about these mistakes?

## Question #1

To what king was the prophet Nathan speaking when he pointed out his sin with the words, "Thou art the man"?

a) Saul
b) David
c) Solomon
d) Jeroboam

## Question #2

The king who threw Daniel into the lions' den couldn't change the bad law he'd passed because:

a) he didn't want to
b) the people who tricked him into it wouldn't let him
c) he thought it would make him look weak
d) the law of the land said he couldn't

## Question #3

According to the Gospel writer Mark, Peter was told that he would deny Jesus three times before the cock crowed how many times?

a) once
b) twice
c) three times
d) four times

## Question #4

Moses wasn't allowed to go into the promised land because:

a) he had cursed his sister
b) he was afraid
c) he let the people turn away when they first got there
d) he struck a rock for water instead of speaking to it

## Question #5

When Miriam spoke against Moses, she was struck with leprosy for:

a) seven days
b) forty days
c) a year
d) the rest of her life

## Question #6

What man thought the king was going to honor him and instead ended up having to honor his worst enemy?

a) Haman
b) Mordecai
c) Absalom
d) Ahab

## Question #7

Why did the Lord finally reject Saul from being king?

a) Saul prophesied with the prophets
b) Saul tried to kill David
c) Saul rejected the word of the Lord
d) Saul went to the witch of Endor

## Question #8

When Elisha's servant lied to Naaman and took gifts from him, the servant was struck with:

a) blindness
b) deafness
c) muteness
d) Naaman's leprosy

## Question #9

When Nebuchadnezzar claimed glory for himself instead of honoring God, he became mad and:

a) tore his clothes
b) lived like a wild animal
c) lived in a cave
d) both b and c

## Question #10

When Herod allowed the people to say that his voice was the voice of a god, the angel of the Lord struck him:

a) blind
b) deaf
c) mute
d) dead

# HUMBLING EXPERIENCES ANSWERS

1. b) David (2 Samuel 12:7)
2. d) the law of the land said he couldn't (Daniel 6:7–15)
3. b) twice (Mark 14:72)
4. d) he struck a rock for water instead of speaking to it (Numbers 20:7–12)
5. a) seven days (Numbers 12:1–2, 14–15)
6. a) Haman (Esther 6:6–11)
7. c) Saul rejected the word of the Lord (1 Samuel 15:26)
8. d) Naaman's leprosy (2 Kings 5:20–27)
9. b) lived like a wild animal (Daniel 4:24–25, 30–33)
10. d) dead (Acts 12:20–23)

**So, how did you do?**

# CITIES

When studying the Bible, it helps to understand the geography of the Middle East. Many places are very important to biblical history. The Bible says that unless the Lord keeps the city, the watchman wakes in vain (Psalm 127:1). Some of the following cities were dedicated to the Lord, and some tried to exist without Him. Which of these cities do you recognize?

### Question #1

The city of Babel and the city of Nineveh were both built by:

a) Adam
b) Seth
c) Cain
d) Nimrod

### Question #2

Of the following four cities, which *two* were referred to as the city of David?

a) Zion
b) Bethlehem
c) Samaria
d) Shiloh

### Question #3

Which of the following is *not* one of the foundation stones of the New Jerusalem?

a) sapphire
b) diamond
c) topaz
d) amethyst

## Question #4

What prophet had a vision of a city whose name was "The Lord is there"?

a) Ezekiel
b) Jeremiah
c) Isaiah
d) Daniel

## Question #5

The shortest sermon in the Bible consists of eight words: "Yet forty days, and ___________ shall be overthrown." To what city was this sermon preached?

a) Babylon
b) Sodom
c) Nineveh
d) Gomorrah

## Question #6

When Naomi returned from afar with Ruth, to which city did they go?

a) Jerusalem
b) Nazareth
c) Jericho
d) Bethlehem

## Question #7

Which of the following was *not* a city that Lot lived in?

a) Sodom
b) Gomorrah
c) Zoar
d) Ur

## Question #8

Samson carried off the gates of the city of:

a) Gaza
b) Joppa
c) Ashkelon
d) Jericho

## Question #9

What city was Saul traveling to when he was struck by the light of Jesus?

a) Jerusalem
b) Damascus
c) Corinth
d) Joppa

## Question #10

In what city did Jesus speak to the woman at the well?

a) Jericho
b) Joppa
c) Sychar
d) Caesarea

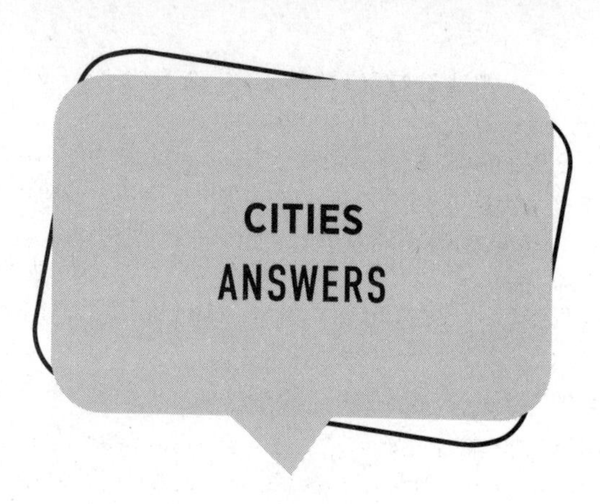


1. d) Nimrod (Genesis 10:8–11)
2. a) Zion (2 Samuel 5:7) and b) Bethlehem (Luke 2:4)
3. b) diamond (Revelation 21:19–20)
4. a) Ezekiel (Ezekiel 48:35)
5. c) Nineveh (Jonah 3:4)
6. d) Bethlehem (Ruth 1:11–19)
7. b) Gomorrah (Genesis 13:12; 19:22–23; 11:31)
8. a) Gaza (Judges 16:1–3)
9. b) Damascus (Acts 9:3–4)
10. c) Sychar (John 4:5–7)

**So, how did you do?**

# THE WORD OF GOD

The Bible itself is the Word of God, and it describes the Word of God in many different ways. Each description helps us understand a different aspect of God's Word and how it relates to us. With which of the following descriptions are you familiar?

### Question #1

There is one psalm in the Bible in which each verse contains a reference to God's Word as His law. That psalm is:

a) Psalm 1
b) Psalm 19
c) Psalm 23
d) Psalm 119

### Question #2

In the parable of the sower, the Word of God is likened to:

a) the sower
b) fertilizer
c) the seed
d) the receptive ground

### Question #3

In the list of the armor of God in Ephesians 6, the Word of God is the:

a) breastplate
b) helmet
c) shield
d) sword

## Question #4

Which Gospel begins by saying the Word was in the beginning with God and was God?

a) Matthew
b) Mark
c) Luke
d) John

## Question #5

Hebrews 4:12 says the Word of God is:

a) quick
b) powerful
c) sharper than a two-edged sword
d) all of the above

## Question #6

Jeremiah 23:29 says the Word of God is like a:

a) fire
b) hammer
c) rock
d) both a and b

## Question #7

What does Hebrews 11:3 say was framed by the Word of God?

a) the worlds
b) the heavens
c) mankind
d) all of the above

### Question #8

Psalm 119:105 says the Word of God is a:

a) river

b) lamp

c) rock

d) path

### Question #9

God said that when His Word goes out, it will not return:

a) void

b) again

c) ever

d) to heaven

### Question #10

How does 2 Timothy 3:16 say scripture was given?

a) for our blessing

b) by inspiration of God

c) in great mystery

d) to angels and men

## THE WORD OF GOD
## ANSWERS

1. d) Psalm 119
2. c) the seed (Luke 8:11)
3. d) sword (Ephesians 6:17)
4. d) John (John 1:1)
5. d) all of the above
6. d) both a and b
7. a) the worlds
8. b) lamp
9. a) void (Isaiah 55:11)
10. b) by inspiration of God

**So, how did you do?**

# ANGELS

"Be not forgetful to entertain strangers: for thereby some have entertained angels unawares" (Hebrews 13:2). Angels appeared to various people in the Bible. Sometimes the people knew they were angels, sometimes not. Are you aware of the following angels?

## Question #1

What man's donkey saw an angel and spoke?

a) Barak
b) Balak
c) Balaam
d) Belshazzar

## Question #2

Which of the following is *not* reported to have seen a host of angels?

a) Jacob
b) Peter
c) shepherds at Bethlehem
d) John

## Question #3

What famous judge's parents saw an angel ascend to heaven in a flame?

a) Gideon
b) Deborah
c) Samson
d) Samuel

## Question #4

The cherubim sent to keep people out of the garden of Eden were placed on which side of the garden?

a) north
b) south
c) east
d) west

## Question #5

To which of the following people did the angel Gabriel *not* appear?

a) Mary
b) Daniel
c) Zacharias
d) Paul

## Question #6

In Revelation 10:5–6 an angel declared that:

a) the kingdom had come
b) Jesus is King of Kings
c) there should be time no longer
d) all of the above

## Question #7

When Isaiah saw the seraphim, how many wings did each one have?

a) two
b) four
c) six
d) eight

## Question #8

The angels carved on the golden top of the ark of the covenant were:

a) cherubim
b) seraphim
c) both cherubim and seraphim
d) neither cherubim nor seraphim

## Question #9

How many angels went to save Lot from the destruction of his city?

a) two
b) three
c) seven
d) ten

## Question #10

Hebrews 2:7 says that God made man:

a) rulers over angels
b) higher than the angels
c) lower than the angels
d) equal with the angels

1. c) Balaam (Numbers 22:22–23)
2. b) Peter (Genesis 28:10–12; Luke 2:8–14; Revelation 7:11)
3. c) Samson (Judges 13:20, 24)
4. c) east (Genesis 3:24)
5. d) Paul (Luke 1:26–27; Daniel 8:15–16; Luke 1:18–19)
6. c) there should be time no longer
7. c) six (Isaiah 6:2)
8. a) cherubim (Exodus 37:1, 7)
9. a) two (Genesis 19:1)
10. c) lower than the angels

**So, how did you do?**

# RUTH AND ESTHER

Only two books of the Bible are named for women. Like all of the Bible's stories, these two stories are important. What do you know about these two extraordinary women?

### Question #1

Ruth was from:

a) Edom
b) Moab
c) Ammon
d) Tyre

### Question #2

Ruth's mother-in-law was:

a) Naomi
b) Orpah
c) Rahab
d) both a and c

### Question #3

Boaz was Naomi's:

a) son
b) kinsman
c) brother-in-law
d) grandfather

## Question #4

When Boaz first saw Ruth, she was:

a) cooking
b) washing clothes
c) planting a garden
d) gleaning

## Question #5

In order to show that he would allow Boaz to marry Ruth, a more closely related man:

a) shook hands
b) winked
c) took off his shoe
d) turned in a circle three times

## Question #6

The name of the queen who preceded Esther was:

a) Vashti
b) Jezebel
c) Sheba
d) Candace

## Question #7

If someone went to King Ahasuerus unannounced, he or she would be killed unless the king:

a) smiled
b) said "Peace"
c) held out his scepter
d) motioned with his hand

## Question #8

Esther's enemy Haman was:

a) a businessman
b) a pagan priest
c) the king's second in command
d) a general

## Question #9

In order to expose Haman's plot, Esther:

a) threw herself at the king's feet
b) invited the king and Haman to a banquet
c) got Mordecai an audience with the king
d) both a and b

## Question #10

A feast was instituted to celebrate the defeat of Haman's plot. It was called the feast of:

a) Tabernacles
b) Esther
c) Purim
d) Mordecai

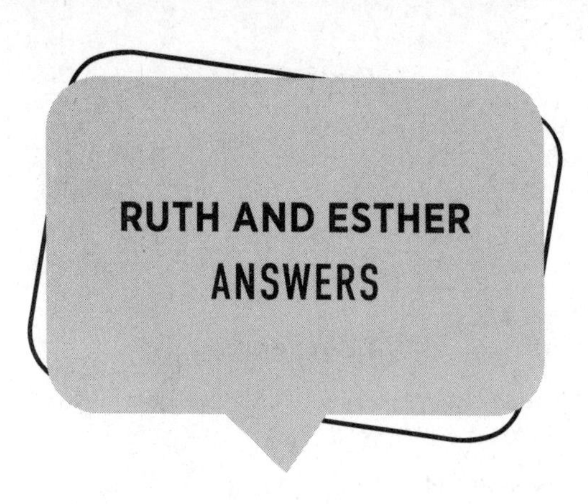

# RUTH AND ESTHER ANSWERS

1. b) Moab (Ruth 1:4)
2. d) both a and c (Ruth 1:2–4; Matthew 1:5)
3. b) kinsman (Ruth 2:1)
4. d) gleaning (Ruth 2:2–4)
5. c) took off his shoe (Ruth 4:8)
6. a) Vashti (Esther 1:9)
7. c) held out his scepter (Esther 4:11)
8. c) the king's second in command (Esther 3:1)
9. b) invited the king and Haman to a banquet (Esther 5:7–8)
10. c) Purim (Esther 9:26)

**So, how did you do?**

# MOUNTAINS

Mountains are plentiful in the geography of the Bible. Many important events took place on or near a mountain. Which of these mountains and events are you familiar with?

## Question #1

God gave Moses the Ten Commandments on Mount:

a) Sinai
b) Pisgah
c) Moriah
d) Zion

## Question #2

Elijah called down fire from heaven to defeat the prophets of Baal on what mountain?

a) Horeb
b) Carmel
c) Hor
d) Moriah

## Question #3

When God showed Moses all of the promised land, He took Moses up on Mount:

a) Sinai
b) Horeb
c) Pisgah
d) Moriah

### Question #4

When God tested Abraham, He told Abraham to take Isaac up on Mount:

a) Zion
b) Moriah
c) Horeb
d) Sinai

### Question #5

The garden of Gethsemane was on:

a) the Mount of Olives
b) Mount Hermon
c) Mount Calvary
d) Mount Zion

### Question #6

Which of the following mountains was called the "mountain of God" or the "mount [or "mountain"] of the LORD"?

a) Zion
b) Sinai
c) Horeb
d) all of the above

### Question #7

Mount Calvary is also called Golgotha, which means:

a) "death"
b) "burning"
c) "shame"
d) "skull"

## Question #8

Jesus was transfigured on:

a) Mount Calvary
b) an unnamed high mountain
c) the Mount of Olives
d) Mount Zion

## Question #9

Upon what mountain was Moses when he saw the burning bush?

a) Sinai
b) Horeb
c) Tabor
d) Midian

## Question #10

Which of the following tribes of Israel had a mountain named for it?

a) Reuben
b) Gad
c) Ephraim
d) Dan

1. a) Sinai (Exodus 19:18–20:17)
2. b) Carmel (1 Kings 18:19, 30–38)
3. c) Pisgah (Deuteronomy 34:1–4)
4. b) Moriah (Genesis 22:1–2)
5. a) the Mount of Olives (Matthew 26:36; Luke 22:39)
6. d) all of the above (Isaiah 2:3; Numbers 10:12, 3; Exodus 3:1)
7. d) "skull" (Matthew 27:33)
8. b) an unnamed high mountain (Matthew 17:1–2)
9. b) Horeb (Exodus 3:1–4)
10. c) Ephraim (1 Samuel 1:1)

**So, how did you do?**

# NAMES OF THE LORD

Romans 10:13 says, "Whosoever shall call upon the name of the Lord shall be saved." The Lord tells us many of His different names because each of them speaks to a different aspect of His character. Knowing His names helps us to know God better. How well do you know these names of the Lord?

### Question #1

To whom was God speaking when He said, "Say unto the children of Israel, I AM hath sent me unto you"?

a) Aaron
b) Moses
c) Joshua
d) Elijah

### Question #2

Who called the Lord "Thou God seest me"?

a) Sarai
b) Abram
c) Hagar
d) Ishmael

### Question #3

To whom was God speaking when He said, "I am the Almighty God"?

a) Moses
b) Aaron
c) Abram
d) Pharaoh

## Question #4

When Moses told the children of Israel to remember the days of old, he referred to the Lord as:

a) the Most High
b) the Ancient of Days
c) the Lord of Lords
d) the Lord above all

## Question #5

Which of the Ten Commandments tells us not to take our Lord's name in vain?

a) the first
b) the second
c) the third
d) the fourth

## Question #6

Which of the following names is *not* in the list found in Isaiah 9:6?

a) Bright and Morning Star
b) Prince of Peace
c) Mighty God
d) Counsellor

## Question #7

"KING OF KINGS, AND LORD OF LORDS" was written on Jesus':

a) vesture and thigh
b) shield
c) sword
d) breastplate

## Question #8

Which of the following names means "God with us"?

a) Jesus
b) Elohim
c) Emmanuel
d) Elyon

## Question #9

Philippians 2:9 says that God gave Jesus:

a) the name Jesus
b) the name above every name
c) a secret name
d) b and c

## Question #10

Who said, "I know that my redeemer liveth"?

a) David
b) Job
c) Moses
d) Isaiah

# NAMES OF THE LORD ANSWERS

1. b) Moses (Exodus 3:14)
2. c) Hagar (Genesis 16:8, 13)
3. c) Abram (Genesis 17:1)
4. a) the Most High (Deuteronomy 31:30; 32:8)
5. c) the third (Exodus 20:7)
6. a) Bright and Morning Star
7. a) vesture and thigh (Revelation 19:16)
8. c) Emmanuel (Matthew 1:23)
9. b) the name above every name
10. b) Job (Job 19:1, 25)

**So, how did you do?**

# JESUS' CRUCIFIXION AND RESURRECTION

Galatians 2:20 says, "I am crucified with Christ: nevertheless I live; yet not I, but Christ liveth in me." Jesus' crucifixion and resurrection are the most important events ever to happen in this world. What do you know about these crucial events?

## Question #1

The week before His crucifixion, Jesus entered Jerusalem and was greeted with:

a) shouts of "hosanna"
b) strewn garments
c) waving of tree branches
d) all of the above

## Question #2

The signal of Jesus' betrayal was a:

a) handshake
b) pointed finger
c) slap in the face
d) kiss

## Question #3

Jesus was tried before:

a) Caiaphas
b) Pilate
c) Herod
d) all of the above

## Question #4

Who helped Jesus to carry His cross?

a) Peter
b) a Roman soldier
c) Simon of Cyrene
d) John Mark

## Question #5

The sign Pilate put on Jesus' cross said THE KING OF THE JEWS in how many languages?

a) one
b) two
c) three
d) four

## Question #6

Who gave his own tomb for Jesus' burial?

a) Nicodemus
b) Joseph of Arimathea
c) Peter
d) Lazarus

## Question #7

How many Marys stood at the foot of Jesus' cross?

a) one
b) two
c) three
d) four

## Question #8

Who came first to the tomb on the first day of the week?

a) Peter
b) John
c) Mary, Jesus' mother
d) Mary Magdalene

## Question #9

Who rolled the stone away from Jesus' grave?

a) an angel
b) the women
c) Jesus' disciples
d) Roman soldiers

## Question #10

What was left in the tomb?

a) nothing
b) the linen clothes
c) some spices
d) an angel

# JESUS' CRUCIFIXION AND RESURRECTION

## ANSWERS

1. d) all of the above (Matthew 21:8–9)
2. d) kiss (Matthew 26:49)
3. d) all of the above (Matthew 26:57; 27:11–13; Luke 23:7)
4. c) Simon of Cyrene (Matthew 27:32)
5. c) three (Luke 23:38; John 19:19)
6. b) Joseph of Arimathea (Matthew 27:57–60)
7. c) three (John 19:25)
8. d) Mary Magdalene (John 20:1)
9. a) an angel (Matthew 28:2)
10. b) the linen clothes (John 20:6)

**So, how did you do?**

# PRIESTS

God instituted the priesthood. He chose the tribe of Levi because they were the only ones who stood with Moses to punish those worshipping the golden calf. The only book of the Bible named for a tribe of Israel is Leviticus, which describes the duties of the priests. Today we Christians are God's royal priesthood. What do you know about the biblical priests?

### Question #1

When Samuel was dedicated to service in the house of the Lord, the priest he served was:

a) Zadok
b) Eli
c) Eleazar
d) Melchizedek

### Question #2

When Aaron died, what was the name of his son who became high priest?

a) Eleazar
b) Phinehas
c) Joshua
d) Caleb

### Question #3

Melchizedek was a priest of:

a) Jerusalem
b) Baal
c) the most high God
d) Israel

## Question #4

Which apostle wrote a book of the Bible that describes all believers as a royal priesthood?

a) Paul
b) Peter
c) James
d) John

## Question #5

When the Israelites returned to Jerusalem from the Babylonian captivity, the high priest was:

a) Ezra
b) Nehemiah
c) Joshua
d) Zerubbabel

## Question #6

David put the two priests Abiathar and Zadok in charge of:

a) the temple service
b) bringing the ark of the covenant to Jerusalem
c) the temple singers
d) all the other priests

## Question #7

Hebrews says that Jesus is our high priest forever according to the order of:

a) Moses
b) Aaron
c) Levi
d) Melchizedek

## Question #8

In Jesus' day a curious situation occurred in which two men were referred to as being the high priest. The two men were:

a) Annas and Caiaphas
b) Caiaphas and Zecharias
c) Annas and Zecharias
d) Caiaphas and Gamaliel

## Question #9

Which of the following was *not* a part of the outfit priests were to wear?

a) ephod
b) turban
c) breastplate
d) gloves

## Question #10

How often could the high priest enter the holy of holies, where the ark of the covenant was?

a) once a year
b) on holy feast days
c) on the sabbath
d) twice a year

## PRIESTS ANSWERS

1. b) Eli (1 Samuel 1:20–25)
2. a) Eleazar (Deuteronomy 10:6)
3. c) the most high God (Genesis 14:18)
4. b) Peter (1 Peter 2:9)
5. c) Joshua (Haggai 1:1–2)
6. b) bringing the ark of the covenant to Jerusalem (2 Samuel 15:29)
7. d) Melchizedek (Hebrews 6:20)
8. a) Annas and Caiaphas (Luke 3:2)
9. d) gloves (Exodus 28:4–39)
10. a) once a year (Hebrews 9:6–7)

**So, how did you do?**

# PLAGUES

When God was ready to deliver His people from slavery in Egypt, He sent Moses to Pharaoh. But Pharaoh refused to let God's people go. Some scholars say that each of the plagues was directed against a specific Egyptian god or goddess so that God could show His supremacy over all phony gods. What do you know about the plagues? Can you name all ten plagues?

## Question #1

Which of the following plagues could the Egyptian magicians *not* duplicate?

a) water to blood
b) rods turned into snakes
c) frogs
d) lice

## Question #2

How many plagues did God send against the Egyptians?

a) three
b) seven
c) ten
d) forty

## Question #3

To keep the angel of death from killing their firstborn, the Israelites anointed their doorposts and lintels with:

a) hyssop
b) myrrh
c) blood
d) frankincense

## Question #4

Which of the following plagues is *not* paralleled in the plagues of the tribulation in the book of Revelation?

a) locusts
b) darkness
c) hail and fire
d) boils

## Question #5

Out of the following list, which plague occurred first?

a) boils
b) flies
c) frogs
d) locusts

## Question #6

God told Aaron to stretch out his rod so that the dust of the land would become:

a) locusts
b) flies
c) a cloud of darkness
d) lice

## Question #7

The Bible repeatedly says that Pharaoh:

a) loved his power
b) closed his mind
c) hardened his heart
d) closed his ears

## Question #8

The last plague—death of the firstborn—resulted in what major celebration for the Israelites?

a) the Day of Atonement
b) the Feast of Tabernacles
c) Passover
d) the Feast of Trumpets

## Question #9

God visited the plagues upon Egypt:

a) because He was angry at the Egyptians
b) because He was angry with Pharaoh
c) so that the Egyptians would know that He is Lord
d) so that future generations would fear

## Question #10

How many days did the plague of darkness last?

a) one
b) two
c) three
d) four

# PLAGUES ANSWERS

1. d) lice (Exodus 8:16–19)
2. c) ten (Exodus 7:20; 8:6, 17, 24; 9:6, 10, 23; 10:13, 22; 12:29)
3. c) blood (Exodus 12:7, 13)
4. d) boils (Revelation 8:7; 9:2–3)
5. c) frogs (Exodus 8:2)
6. d) lice (Exodus 8:16)
7. c) hardened his heart (Exodus 8:15, 32; 9:34; 10:1; 11:10)
8. c) Passover (Exodus 12:13–14)
9. c) so that the Egyptians would know that He is Lord (Exodus 7:5)
10. c) three (Exodus 10:22)

**So, how did you do?**

# TABERNACLE AND TEMPLE

Hebrews 8:5 says that God told Moses to make the tabernacle according to the pattern shown to him on the mount. The temple was patterned after the tabernacle but as a permanent dwelling. How much do you know about the tabernacle and the temple?

### Question #1

Which of the following was *not* one of the colors of the tabernacle curtains?

a) blue
b) scarlet
c) purple
d) white

### Question #2

Which of the following was *not* placed in the holy of holies?

a) table of showbread
b) altar of incense
c) a bronze basin for washing
d) golden lampstand

### Question #3

Who carried the tabernacle and its furnishings?

a) the Levites
b) the Gadites
c) the Reubenites
d) the Ephraimites

## Question #4

When the Israelites camped, the tabernacle was set up:

a) to the north of the camp
b) to the south of the camp
c) to the east of the camp
d) in the middle of the camp

## Question #5

The glory of the Lord filled the tabernacle as:

a) a pillar of cloud
b) a pillar of fire
c) lightning
d) both a and b

## Question #6

Who built the first temple?

a) Moses
b) Solomon
c) Samuel
d) Hezekiah

## Question #7

Why did God tell David that he couldn't build the temple?

a) because he didn't have the right building materials
b) because he sinned with Bathsheba
c) because he had shed much blood
d) because he was too old

## Question #8

According to 1 Chronicles 22:1–5, which of the following was *not* a material gathered to build the temple?

a) iron
b) brass (or bronze)
c) stone
d) gold

## Question #9

Jesus cleansed the temple of:

a) money changers
b) animals
c) Pharisees
d) priests

## Question #10

When Jesus died, the veil in the temple was torn in two from:

a) bottom to top
b) top to bottom
c) right to left
d) left to right

# TABERNACLE AND TEMPLE
## ANSWERS

1. d) white (Exodus 26:1)
2. c) a bronze basin for washing (Exodus 30:18)
3. a) the Levites (Numbers 1:50)
4. d) in the middle of the camp (Numbers 2:17)
5. d) both a and b (Exodus 40:38)
6. b) Solomon (2 Chronicles 2:1)
7. c) because he had shed much blood (1 Chronicles 22:8)
8. d) gold
9. a) money changers (Matthew 21:12)
10. b) top to bottom (Mark 15:38)

**So, how did you do?**

# WHERE IS THIS FOUND?

In addition to quoting familiar verses, some people can quote famous stories or passages. Do you know where the following are found?

## Question #1

Which two books of the New Testament record what we know as "the Lord's Prayer"?

a) Matthew and Luke
b) Matthew and Mark
c) Matthew and John
d) Matthew and Acts

## Question #2

What verse in the Bible is commonly referred to as "the Golden Rule"?

a) John 3:16
b) Matthew 7:12
c) Luke 2:52
d) Mark 16:18

## Question #3

Where is the Bible's description of the virtuous woman?

a) Psalm 19
b) Ecclesiastes 3
c) Proverbs 31
d) Song of Solomon 1

## Question #4

What book of the Bible is characterized by the phrase "vanity of vanities; all is vanity"?

a) Job
b) Ecclesiastes
c) Micah
d) Hosea

## Question #5

What book of the Bible contains the story of David and Goliath?

a) 1 Samuel
b) 2 Samuel
c) 1 Kings
d) 2 Kings

## Question #6

What book of the Bible contains the story of Noah and the flood?

a) Genesis
b) Exodus
c) Leviticus
d) Numbers

## Question #7

The story of the prodigal son is found in which Gospel?

a) Matthew
b) Mark
c) Luke
d) John

## Question #8

Where can you find the saying "They shall beat their swords into plowshares"?

a) Job 40:1
b) Jeremiah 1:5
c) Amos 3:3
d) Isaiah 2:4

## Question #9

Where can we find the foolish man building his house upon the sand?

a) Matthew 7:26
b) Mark 7:26
c) Luke 7:26
d) John 7:26

## Question #10

Where is the story of Moses in the bulrushes found?

a) Exodus 1
b) Exodus 2
c) Exodus 3
d) Exodus 4

# WHERE IS THIS FOUND?
## ANSWERS

1. a) Matthew and Luke (Matthew 6:9–13; Luke 11:2–4)
2. b) Matthew 7:12
3. c) Proverbs 31
4. b) Ecclesiastes 1:2; 12:8
5. a) 1 Samuel 17
6. a) Genesis 6–9
7. c) Luke 15:11–32
8. d) Isaiah 2:4
9. a) Matthew 7:26
10. b) Exodus 2:2–8

**So, how did you do?**

# JESUS SPEAKING

Everything Jesus said was well worth listening to. He spoke to many thousands of people, but He also spoke to individuals. Jesus was compassionate, kind, loving, and informative. To whom was Jesus speaking when He made the following statements?

## Question #1

"Suffer the little children to come unto me, and forbid them not."

a) their parents
b) His disciples
c) the Pharisees
d) the crowd

## Question #2

"Whosoever liveth and believeth in me shall never die. Believest thou this?"

a) Mary Magdalene
b) the woman at the well
c) Martha
d) His mother

## Question #3

"Woman, why weepest thou?"

a) His mother
b) Mary, the sister of Lazarus
c) Martha
d) Mary Magdalene

## Question #4

"Woman, what have I to do with thee?"

a) the woman at the well
b) the woman with an issue of blood
c) Pilate's wife
d) His mother

## Question #5

"Why persecutest thou me?"

a) the high priest
b) the Pharisees
c) Satan
d) Saul

## Question #6

"What is that to thee? follow thou me."

a) Peter
b) Andrew
c) James
d) John

## Question #7

"Why callest thou me good?"

a) Matthew
b) Nathaniel
c) the rich young ruler
d) Nicodemus

## Question #8

"God is a Spirit: and they that worship him must worship him in spirit and in truth."

a) the Pharisees
b) His disciples
c) the woman at the well
d) Pilate

## Question #9

"Wist ye not that I must be about my Father's business?"

a) His disciples
b) His parents
c) Mary and Martha
d) Philip

## Question #10

"That thou doest, do quickly."

a) Peter
b) John
c) Judas
d) Caiaphas

# JESUS SPEAKING

## ANSWERS

1. b) His disciples (Mark 10:13–14)
2. c) Martha (John 11:24, 26)
3. d) Mary Magdalene (John 20:1, 15)
4. d) His mother (John 2:3–4)
5. d) Saul (Acts 9:4)
6. a) Peter (John 21:21–22)
7. c) the rich young ruler (Matthew 19:17; Luke 18:18–19)
8. c) the woman at the well (John 4:7, 24)
9. b) His parents (Luke 2:41, 49)
10. c) Judas (John 13:26–27)

**So, how did you do?**

# GOD'S FAITHFUL

Hebrews 11:6 says that without faith it is impossible to please God. All of the following people could say with the apostle Paul, "I have fought a good fight, I have finished my course, I have kept the faith" (2 Timothy 4:7). What do you know about these faithful of God?

## Question #1

Of whom does the Bible say, "In all this ____________ sinned not, nor charged God foolishly"?

a) Nehemiah
b) Job
c) John
d) Moses

## Question #2

Shadrach, Meshach, and Abednego were thrown into the fiery furnace because they refused to:

a) pray to the king
b) bow down to the king's statue
c) stop praying to their God
d) all of the above

## Question #3

About whom is the Bible speaking when it says that among men whose thoughts were only evil continually, this person found grace in the eyes of the Lord?

a) Noah
b) Abraham
c) David
d) Moses

## Question #4

About whom was God speaking when He said, "He had another spirit with him, and hath followed me fully"?

a) Job
b) Caleb
c) David
d) Moses

## Question #5

Which of the following is *not* listed by name in Hebrews 11, God's hall of fame for His faithful?

a) Abel
b) Joseph
c) Rahab
d) Elijah

## Question #6

About which of Noah's ancestors does the Bible say he "walked with God" and "God took him"?

a) Seth
b) Methuselah
c) Enoch
d) Lamech

## Question #7

When Abraham proved his faithfulness to God by preparing to sacrifice Isaac, what did God provide as a sacrifice instead?

a) a lamb
b) a bullock
c) a ram
d) a goat

## Question #8

About whom did Jesus say, "I have not found so great faith, no, not in Israel"?

a) John the Baptist
b) the centurion with the sick servant
c) Jairus
d) the man with the demon-possessed son

## Question #9

How many years did Noah spend preparing the ark as God told him?

a) ten
b) fifty
c) seventy-five
d) a hundred

## Question #10

What prophet who devoutly feared God hid one hundred prophets from Jezebel?

a) Elijah
b) Elisha
c) Obadiah
d) Isaiah

# GOD'S FAITHFUL ANSWERS

1. b) Job (Job 1:22)
2. b) bow down to the king's statue (Daniel 3:12)
3. a) Noah (Genesis 6:5, 8)
4. b) Caleb (Numbers 14:24)
5. d) Elijah
6. c) Enoch (Genesis 5:24)
7. c) a ram (Genesis 22:13)
8. b) the centurion with the sick servant (Matthew 8:5, 10–13)
9. d) a hundred (Genesis 5:32; 7:11)
10. c) Obadiah (1 Kings 18:3–4)

**So, how did you do?**

# THE ACTS OF THE APOSTLES

The book of Acts is sometimes called the Acts of the Apostles because it describes a lot of them—in addition to acts of other followers of Jesus. How many of the following are you familiar with?

### Question #1

On the day of Pentecost, who preached the sermon that led a huge number of people to believe in Jesus?

a) John
b) Peter
c) Andrew
d) James

### Question #2

What kind of beggar did Peter and John heal by saying, "Silver and gold have I none; but such as I have I give thee"?

a) blind
b) deaf
c) dumb
d) lame

### Question #3

When Peter told Ananias and Sapphira that they had lied to the Holy Spirit, their punishment was:

a) banishment
b) flogging
c) confession to the whole church
d) death

## Question #4

The first person martyred for being a Christian was:

a) Philip
b) Peter
c) Stephen
d) Paul

## Question #5

Simon, who tried to buy the gift of the Holy Spirit, was a:

a) king
b) councilman
c) sorcerer
d) priest

## Question #6

The person who spoke to the Ethiopian eunuch was:

a) Peter
b) Philip
c) Paul
d) Andrew

## Question #7

Peter was sent to preach to Cornelius, who was a:

a) Gentile
b) devout man
c) centurion
d) all of the above

## Question #8

When Peter was freed from prison by an angel and went to where the Christians had gathered, he was:

a) welcomed
b) left knocking at the door
c) turned away
d) ignored

## Question #9

The man chosen to replace Judas as an apostle was:

a) Paul
b) Silas
c) Barnabas
d) Matthias

## Question #10

Lydia, who was one of the women converted at Philippi, was a seller of:

a) purple
b) pottery
c) rich clothing
d) housewares

## THE ACTS OF THE APOSTLES

## ANSWERS

1. b) Peter (Acts 2:1, 14)
2. d) lame (Acts 3:1–7)
3. d) death (Acts 5:1–10)
4. c) Stephen (Acts 7:59)
5. c) sorcerer (Acts 8:9, 18)
6. b) Philip (Acts 8:26–35)
7. d) all of the above (Acts 10:1–2)
8. b) left knocking at the door (Acts 12:6–16)
9. d) Matthias (Acts 1:20–26)
10. a) purple (Acts 16:14)

**So, how did you do?**

# PARABLES

Jesus said that He spoke in parables to fulfill the prophecy of Isaiah that said the people would hear and not understand (Isaiah 6:9). The parables teach many good lessons, but we have to be willing to be taught. What do you know about these parables?

### Question #1

The parable of the good Samaritan was told to answer what question?

a) "Who is my neighbor?"
b) "What shall I do to inherit eternal life?"
c) "Can a rich man be saved?"
d) "By what authority do you do these things?"

### Question #2

The phrase "Well done, thou good and faithful servant" occurs in the parable of the:

a) sower
b) talents
c) minas
d) vineyard

## Question #3

The parable of the unforgiving servant begins with Jesus saying that we should forgive:

a) a hundred times
b) seven times
c) seventy times seven
d) always

## Question #4

In the parable of the lost sheep, how many sheep did the shepherd leave to search for the lost one?

a) 9
b) 99
c) 199
d) 299

## Question #5

In the parable of the sower, upon how many different types of places did the seed fall?

a) two
b) four
c) seven
d) nine

## Question #6

Which parable includes the phrase "eat, drink, and be merry"?

a) Lazarus and the rich man
b) the rich fool
c) the rich young ruler
d) the wise steward

## Question #7

In the parable of the wise and foolish virgins, how many took no oil with them?

a) three
b) five
c) seven
d) nine

## Question #8

In the parable of the wedding feast, a man is thrown out because:

a) he's not wearing a wedding garment
b) he sat in the place of honor uninvited
c) he wasn't invited to the wedding
d) he was rude to the bridegroom

## Question #9

In the parable of the wheat and tares, the owner of the field ultimately tells his servants to:

a) root out the tares
b) leave the tares alone
c) bind the tares and burn them
d) sow more tares

## Question #10

In one parable Jesus said that no one would light a candle and:

a) hide it under a bushel
b) put it in a secret place
c) let someone blow it out
d) both a and b

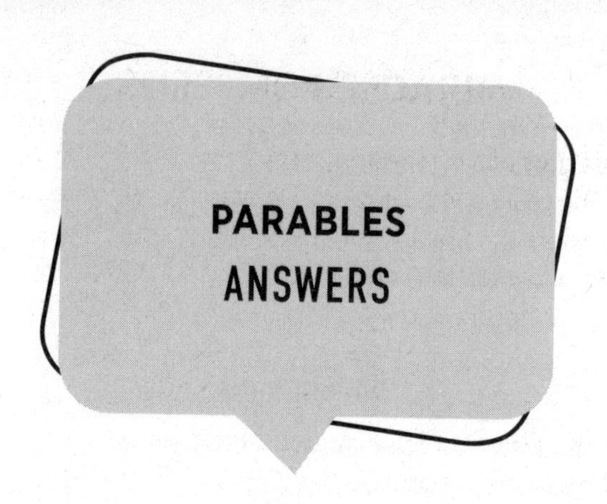


1. a) "Who is my neighbor?" (Luke 10:25–37)
2. b) talents (Matthew 25:14–30)
3. c) seventy times seven (Matthew 18:22–35)
4. b) 99 (Matthew 18:12)
5. b) four (Mark 4:3–8)
6. b) the rich fool (Luke 12:16–21)
7. b) five (Matthew 25:1–13)
8. a) he's not wearing a wedding garment (Matthew 22:11–12)
9. c) bind the tares and burn them (Matthew 13:24–30)
10. d) both a and b (Luke 11:33)

**So, how did you do?**

# MIRACLES OF JESUS

As part of His ministry, Jesus performed miracles. One reason was to prove He was who He said He was—the Son of God. But another reason was to show His love and compassion for His people. What do you know about these miracles?

### Question #1

After Jesus fed the five thousand, He fed another group of four thousand with:

a) five loaves and two fish
b) six loaves and three fish
c) seven loaves and a few fish
d) eight loaves and no fish

### Question #2

When the four thousand were finished eating, how many baskets of leftovers were there?

a) three
b) five
c) seven
d) twelve

### Question #3

When Jesus walked on water, which disciple asked to get out of the boat and walk out with Him?

a) Peter
b) James
c) John
d) Thomas

## Question #4

How long was Lazarus dead before Jesus raised him up again?

a) a few hours
b) a day
c) four days
d) two weeks

## Question #5

Jesus turned the water to wine at:

a) Passover
b) the Last Supper
c) a wedding
d) both a and c

## Question #6

When Jesus healed the ten lepers, how many returned to thank Him?

a) all ten
b) seven
c) three
d) one

## Question #7

When the friends of a paralyzed man couldn't reach Jesus because of the crowd, they:

a) lowered the man down through the roof
b) stood on the edge of the crowd and shouted
c) gave up and went away
d) pushed their way through the crowd

## Question #8

When Jesus healed a man who was blind from birth, what did He put on the man's eyes?

a) clay
b) His hand
c) a scarf
d) nothing

## Question #9

The crippled man Jesus healed at the pool of Bethesda was at the pool because:

a) the waters were healing
b) an angel sometimes appeared
c) it was where he lived
d) both a and b

## Question #10

Jesus once caused a tree to wither to prove a point. What kind of tree was it?

a) olive
b) fig
c) sycamore
d) palm

# MIRACLES OF JESUS ANSWERS

1. c) seven loaves and a few fish (Matthew 15:34–38)
2. c) seven (Matthew 15:37–38)
3. a) Peter (Matthew 14:24–29)
4. c) four days (John 11:14, 39)
5. c) a wedding (John 2:1–10)
6. d) one (Luke 17:12–16)
7. a) lowered the man down through the roof (Mark 2:4)
8. a) clay (John 9:1, 6)
9. d) both a and b (John 5:2–9)
10. b) fig (Mark 11:14, 20)

**So, how did you do?**

# REVELATION

The book of Revelation starts by saying it is a revelation of Jesus Christ given to His servant John. Revelation is full of symbols and strange things that God uses to show Himself to us. How much do you know about this book of the Bible?

### Question #1

Revelation begins with messages to how many churches?

a) three
b) five
c) seven
d) nine

### Question #2

The churches are likened to:

a) stars
b) candlesticks
c) bread
d) salt

### Question #3

Which church did Jesus scold for leaving its "first love"?

a) Ephesus
b) Sardis
c) Philadelphia
d) Smyrna

## Question #4

John saw four horses. The last one was pale and the name of him who rode it was:

a) Hades
b) Apollyon
c) Death
d) Famine

## Question #5

There were 144,000 people who were:

a) those with the mark of the beast
b) God's servants
c) angels
d) martyrs

## Question #6

How many witnesses did God send to Jerusalem?

a) one
b) two
c) three
d) four

## Question #7

What happened to God's witnesses?

a) they were killed and resurrected
b) they ascended into heaven
c) nobody would listen to them
d) nothing

## Question #8

How many beasts stood around God's throne?

a) two
b) four
c) six
d) twenty-four

## Question #9

How many elders were before God's throne?

a) twelve
b) twenty-four
c) thirty-six
d) forty-eight

## Question #10

What did John see descend from the new heaven?

a) a new earth
b) a new sea
c) the new Jerusalem
d) the new army of God

1. c) seven (Revelation 1:4)
2. b) candlesticks (Revelation 1:20)
3. a) Ephesus (Revelation 2 1–4)
4. c) Death (Revelation 6:8)
5. b) God's servants (Revelation 7:3–4)
6. b) two (Revelation 11:3)
7. a) they were killed and resurrected (Revelation 11:3, 7, 11)
8. b) four (Revelation 4:6)
9. b) twenty-four (Revelation 4:10)
10. c) the new Jerusalem (Revelation 21:1–2)

**So, how did you do?**

# NUMBERS

The Bible is full of significant numbers. Some numbers we see repeated over and over, like forty and seven. There is even a book called Numbers. What do you know about the following numbers? (You won't need a calculator, we promise!)

### Question #1

How many prophesying daughters did Philip the evangelist have?

a) one
b) four
c) seven
d) twelve

### Question #2

How many were added to the church on the day of Pentecost?

a) a thousand
b) two thousand
c) three thousand
d) ten thousand

### Question #3

How many foxes did Samson tie together with firebrands to burn his enemies' fields?

a) fifty
b) a hundred
c) three hundred
d) a thousand

## Question #4

How many years were the children of Israel in Egypt?

a) 120
b) 360
c) 430
d) 520

## Question #5

What was the final count of men in Gideon's army?

a) sixty
b) three hundred
c) ten thousand
d) twenty-two thousand

## Question #6

After Noah finished the ark, how many days and nights did it rain?

a) seven
b) ten
c) forty
d) one hundred

## Question #7

How old was Methuselah when he died?

a) 909
b) 929
c) 949
d) 969

## Question #8

How many cities were the Levites given as their inheritance in the promised land?

a) twelve
b) twenty-four
c) thirty-six
d) forty-eight

## Question #9

How many times did the children of Israel march around Jericho?

a) once
b) six times
c) seven times
d) thirteen times

## Question #10

How many years did the children of Israel have to wander in the wilderness?

a) seventeen
b) forty
c) fifty
d) ninety-one

1. b) four (Acts 21:8–9)
2. c) three thousand (Acts 2:1, 41)
3. c) three hundred (Judges 15:4–5)
4. c) 430 (Exodus 12:40)
5. b) three hundred (Judges 7:7)
6. c) forty (Genesis 7:11–12)
7. d) 969 (Genesis 5:27)
8. d) forty-eight (Numbers 35:2, 7)
9. d) thirteen times (Joshua 6:1–4)
10. b) forty (Numbers 14:27, 33)

**So, how did you do?**

# MORE MISCELLANY

Here are some more questions left over from other categories, a little potpourri to test your general knowledge.

## Question #1

When God told Jonah to go preach, where did Jonah try to flee to?

a) Joppa
b) Egypt
c) Tarshish
d) Rome

## Question #2

"The valley of the shadow of death" is mentioned in which psalm?

a) Psalm 1
b) Psalm 23
c) Psalm 119
d) Psalm 150

## Question #3

Which of the following is a place where Satan's temptation of Jesus did *not* occur?

a) the wilderness
b) the sea
c) a mountain
d) the temple

## Question #4

Paul said his missionary companion Luke was a "beloved ___________."

a) historian
b) ship's captain
c) tent maker
d) physician

## Question #5

How many people were on the ark during the flood?

a) two
b) four
c) six
d) eight

## Question #6

What is the only book of the Bible that mentions Lucifer?

a) Revelation
b) Isaiah
c) Ezekiel
d) Daniel

## Question #7

What prophet saw the valley of dry bones?

a) Ezekiel
b) Elijah
c) Elisha
d) Ezra

## Question #8

Who wrote most of the proverbs in the book of Proverbs?

a) David
b) Solomon
c) Moses
d) Isaiah

## Question #9

How did Judas Iscariot die?

a) he hanged himself
b) the earth swallowed him
c) fire fell on him from heaven
d) he was bitten by a poisonous snake

## Question #10

Ecclesiastes 12:13 says the whole duty of man is to:

a) love the Lord with all your heart
b) love your neighbor as yourself
c) fear God and keep His commandments
d) remember now your Creator in the days of your youth

# MORE MISCELLANY ANSWERS

1. c) Tarshish (Jonah 1:1–3)
2. b) Psalm 23 (verse 4)
3. b) the sea (Matthew 4:1–11)
4. d) physician (Colossians 4:14)
5. d) eight (1 Peter 3:20)
6. b) Isaiah (Isaiah 14:12)
7. a) Ezekiel (Ezekiel 37:1)
8. b) Solomon (Proverbs 1:1)
9. a) he hanged himself (Matthew 27:3–5)
10. c) fear God and keep His commandments

**So, how did you do?**

# HUSBANDS AND WIVES

There are many familiar couples in the Bible. Proverbs 18:22 says, "Whoso findeth a wife findeth a good thing." Some of the biblical couples we're familiar with show the truth of this verse. But some of them seem to defy this verse's logic. What do you know about the following husbands and wives?

### Question #1

When David took Bathsheba, she was the wife of:

a) Nathan
b) Zadok
c) Uriah
d) Uzziah

### Question #2

What wife helped trick her husband into giving his blessing to the wrong son?

a) Rebekah
b) Rachel
c) Leah
d) Jezebel

### Question #3

Which of the following wives was *not* found by a well?

a) Rebekah
b) Rachel
c) Bathsheba
d) Zipporah

## Question #4

Lot's wife was turned into a pillar of salt because:

a) she refused to leave the city
b) she was disrespectful to her husband
c) she had committed adultery
d) she looked back while the city was being destroyed

## Question #5

What man's wife told him to curse God and die?

a) Esau
b) Job
c) David
d) Ishmael

## Question #6

The husband-and-wife team of Aquila and Priscilla, who let Paul live with them, were:

a) clothing makers
b) tent makers
c) cheese makers
d) wine makers

## Question #7

After David slew two hundred Philistines, King Saul gave his daughter ____________ to David for a wife.

a) Bathsheba
b) Abigail
c) Michal
d) Tamar

## Question #8

When Nabal churlishly refused to help David and his men, Nabal's wife, ___________, interceded.

a) Abishag
b) Abigail
c) Ahinoam
d) Adah

## Question #9

Who blamed his wife and God for a sin he committed?

a) David
b) Moses
c) Adam
d) Solomon

## Question #10

What happened to Samson's first wife?

a) she died
b) she was given to another man
c) he divorced her
d) she refused to leave her father's house

# HUSBANDS AND WIVES ANSWERS

1. c) Uriah (2 Samuel 11:3)
2. a) Rebekah (Genesis 27:1–19)
3. c) Bathsheba (Genesis 24:10–16; 29:9–10; Exodus 2:16–21)
4. d) she looked back while the city was being destroyed (Genesis 19:17, 26)
5. b) Job (Job 2:9)
6. b) tent makers (Acts 18:1–3)
7. c) Michal (1 Samuel 18:27)
8. b) Abigail (1 Samuel 25:14, 18–20, 23–31)
9. c) Adam (Genesis 3:12)
10. b) she was given to another man (Judges 14:20)

**So, how did you do?**

# THE APOSTLE PAUL

Perhaps Paul was the apostle who had the most influence on the early church. God certainly used him mightily, especially to bring the gospel to the Gentiles. How much do you know about Paul's activities?

### Question #1

How many books of the Bible did Paul write?

a) one
b) nine
c) eleven
d) thirteen

### Question #2

Paul was a very educated man. To which Jewish group did he belong?

a) the Sadducees
b) the scribes
c) the Pharisees
d) the Sanhedrin

### Question #3

How many days was Paul blind after his Damascus Road experience?

a) one
b) two
c) three
d) four

## Question #4

Paul wrote to Philemon concerning:

a) a servant
b) the law
c) salvation
d) grace

## Question #5

Paul had a vision of a man from:

a) Rome
b) Macedonia
c) Philippi
d) Galatia

## Question #6

Paul and Silas were beaten and put into prison in:

a) Philippi
b) Ephesus
c) Colosse
d) Rome

## Question #7

Before Paul traveled with Silas, his missionary companion was:

a) Peter
b) Philip
c) Barnabas
d) Stephen

## Question #8

Who said to Paul, "Almost thou persuadest me to be a Christian"?

a) Festus
b) Felix
c) Agrippa
d) Caesar

## Question #9

When Paul was being tried, he appealed to:

a) his fellow Christians
b) Peter
c) the church council
d) Caesar

## Question #10

The young man who fell out of the window when Paul was preaching was:

a) Timothy
b) Titus
c) Eutychus
d) John Mark

# THE APOSTLE PAUL ANSWERS

1. d) thirteen: Romans, 1 and 2 Corinthians, Galatians, Ephesians, Philippians, Colossians, 1 and 2 Thessalonians, 1 and 2 Timothy, Titus, and Philemon. (Though the King James Bible ascribes Hebrews to Paul, Hebrews doesn't specifically identify its author.)
2. c) the Pharisees (Philippians 3:4–5)
3. c) three (Acts 9:8–9)
4. a) a servant (Philemon 10, 16)
5. b) Macedonia (Acts 16:9)
6. a) Philippi (Acts 16:12, 23–24)
7. c) Barnabas (Acts 13:2–3)
8. c) Agrippa (Acts 26:28)
9. d) Caesar (Acts 25:10–12)
10. c) Eutychus (Acts 20:9)

**So, how did you do?**

# GOD'S BATTLES

Exodus 14:14 says, "The Lord shall fight for you, and ye shall hold your peace." While, indeed, all our battles are the Lord's, what do you know about these specific battles where God did all the fighting?

### Question #1

In one of the battles that God fought for Joshua, God rained ____________ down from heaven upon the enemy.

a) eagles
b) stones
c) walls of water
d) fire

### Question #2

What enemy was surrounding Jerusalem when the angel of the Lord smote and killed 185,000 men in one night?

a) the Philistines
b) the Babylonians
c) the Midianites
d) the Assyrians

### Question #3

When Elisha's servant was afraid, Elisha prayed and the servant saw:

a) horses and chariots of fire
b) angels with swords
c) a huge dust cloud
d) a pillar of fire

## Question #4

What was the last thing God had the children of Israel do before the walls of Jericho fell down?

a) march around the city
b) blow trumpets
c) sing
d) shout

## Question #5

When the children of Israel fought the Amalekites, they won as long as Aaron and Hur:

a) prayed
b) offered sacrifices
c) held up Moses' hands
d) sang

## Question #6

What king won a battle by sending singers instead of soldiers—just as God had told him to do?

a) Jehoshaphat
b) Hezekiah
c) Josiah
d) Joash

## Question #7

God told Moses that He would send what type of insects to drive the Hivites, Canaanites, and Hittites out of the promised land?

a) locusts
b) hornets
c) ants
d) lice

## Question #8

When Gideon did what God told him to do, the battle was won because God:

a) caused the enemy to kill one another
b) sent chariots of fire to destroy the enemy
c) washed the enemy away with a flood
d) caused the earth to open up and swallow the enemy

## Question #9

When the angels went to save Lot, they:

a) struck the men of his city blind
b) told Lot to get ready to leave
c) led him out by the hand
d) all of the above

## Question #10

When God led the children of Israel out of Egypt, how did He destroy the Egyptian army?

a) by fire
b) by water
c) with hail
d) the earth swallowed them

1. b) stones (Joshua 10:5–11)
2. d) the Assyrians (2 Kings 19:35)
3. a) horses and chariots of fire (2 Kings 6:17)
4. d) shout (Joshua 6:1, 20)
5. c) held up Moses' hands (Exodus 17:10–12)
6. a) Jehoshaphat (2 Chronicles 20:1, 21–22)
7. b) hornets (Exodus 23:28)
8. a) caused the enemy to kill one another (Judges 7:9–22)
9. d) all of the above (Genesis 19:1, 11, 15–16)
10. b) by water (Exodus 14:26–30)

**So, how did you do?**

# FILLED WITH THE SPIRIT

Many people in the Bible were filled with the Spirit of God, who empowered them to do great things for Him. Tragically, some, like King Saul and Samson, caused the Spirit to depart from them. But the following stayed true to their callings and were blessed. How much do you know about them?

## Question #1

Bezalel was the person whom God handpicked and gave the skills to:

a) lead His army
b) write some of the psalms
c) build the tabernacle
d) lead the temple singers

## Question #2

God's Spirit came upon David when:

a) David played his harp
b) Samuel anointed him
c) David was crowned king
d) David killed Goliath

## Question #3

Jesus said the Spirit of the Lord had anointed Him to:

a) preach
b) heal
c) liberate the oppressed
d) all of the above

## Question #4

When the Spirit of the Lord came upon Zechariah, the son of Jehoiada, the people did not like what he said, so they:

a) banished him
b) stoned him
c) drowned him
d) buried him alive

## Question #5

Elisabeth was filled with the Spirit, and when Mary greeted her:

a) Elisabeth's baby leaped in her womb
b) Elisabeth blessed Mary
c) Elisabeth fixed Mary a meal
d) both a and b

## Question #6

Who said, "I was in the Spirit on the Lord's day"?

a) John
b) Peter
c) Jesus
d) Paul

## Question #7

When the Holy Spirit was poured out on the Gentiles, the Jews:

a) were dismayed
b) were astonished
c) didn't believe it
d) didn't care

## Question #8

One person asked for a double portion of the Spirit, and it was granted to him. That person was:

a) Elisha
b) Elijah
c) Isaiah
d) David

## Question #9

Who was filled with the Spirit and saw Jesus standing at the right hand of God in heaven?

a) Paul
b) John
c) Stephen
d) Peter

## Question #10

One list of the gifts of the Spirit is in 1 Corinthians:

a) chapter 11
b) chapter 12
c) chapter 13
d) chapter 14

# FILLED WITH THE SPIRIT ANSWERS

1. c) build the tabernacle (Exodus 35:4–33)
2. b) Samuel anointed him (1 Samuel 16:13)
3. d) all of the above (Luke 4:18–19)
4. b) stoned him (2 Chronicles 24:20–21)
5. d) both a and b (Luke 1:41–42)
6. a) John (Revelation 1:10)
7. b) were astonished (Acts 10:44–45)
8. a) Elisha (2 Kings 2:9)
9. c) Stephen (Acts 7:55–59)
10. b) chapter 12

**So, how did you do?**

# THE BIRTH AND EARLY DAYS OF JESUS

Almost everyone loves Christmas—but it's so much more than just gifts and family gatherings. How much do you know about the birth of Jesus and the early days of His life on earth?

### Question #1

What Old Testament verse foretold that Jesus would be born in Bethlehem?

a) Isaiah 7:14
b) Micah 5:2
c) Isaiah 9:6–7
d) Joel 2:5

### Question #2

Who was Caesar at the time Jesus was born?

a) Julius
b) Nero
c) Dominican
d) Augustus

### Question #3

Which of the following women is *not* mentioned by name in Jesus' genealogy?

a) Rahab
b) Ruth
c) Bathsheba
d) Tamar

## Question #4

How old was Jesus when He was taken to the temple to be presented?

a) a day
b) eight days
c) a month
d) one year

## Question #5

What sacrifice was given for Jesus' presentation at the temple?

a) a lamb
b) a bullock
c) two turtledoves
d) a goat

## Question #6

Whom did the wise men ask, "Where is he that is born King of the Jews?"

a) the shepherds
b) an angel
c) King Herod
d) the priests

## Question #7

Where did God tell Joseph to take Mary and Jesus to keep them safe?

a) Nazareth
b) Egypt
c) Jerusalem
d) Caesarea

## Question #8

Herod ordered all the children in Bethlehem from the age of ___________ and younger to be killed.

a) six months
b) a year
c) two years
d) five years

## Question #9

Where were Mary and Joseph living before they traveled to Bethlehem for Jesus' birth?

a) Nain
b) Cana
c) Magdala
d) Nazareth

## Question #10

Angels told shepherds near Bethlehem that they would see what sign?

a) the star
b) an archangel
c) the babe lying in a manger
d) sheep and wolves lying side by side

# THE BIRTH AND EARLY DAYS OF JESUS

## ANSWERS

1. b) Micah 5:2
2. d) Augustus (Luke 2:1)
3. c) Bathsheba (Matthew 1:1–16)
4. b) eight days (Luke 2:21–24)
5. c) two turtledoves (Luke 2:24)
6. c) King Herod (Matthew 2:1–3)
7. b) Egypt (Matthew 2:13)
8. c) two years (Matthew 2:16)
9. d) Nazareth (Luke 2:4)
10. c) the babe lying in a manger (Luke 2:8–12)

**So, how did you do?**

# GOD'S GLORY

Our God is an awesome God, and we need to give Him respect and awe for His wondrous works. The Bible is full of descriptions of God's glory. Let us glorify our Lord together.

## Question #1

Psalm 19:1 says, "The ____________ declare the glory of God "

a) worlds
b) nations
c) heavens
d) people

## Question #2

Romans 1:23 says man changed the glory of the incorruptible God into:

a) an image of corruptible man
b) an image of birds
c) an image of creeping things
d) all of the above

## Question #3

The glory of the Lord departed from Israel when:

a) the ark of the covenant was taken
b) they were taken into captivity
c) they refused to go into the promised land
d) they lost their battle

## Question #4

When the glory of the Lord filled the temple Solomon built, the priests:

a) sacrificed a bull
b) had to leave
c) declared a feast
d) burned incense

## Question #5

What did Paul say "every tongue" would do "to the glory of God the Father"?

a) acknowledge the Lord's power
b) speak the truth in love
c) sing psalms, hymns, and spiritual songs
d) confess that Jesus Christ is Lord

## Question #6

"For all have sinned, and come short of the glory of God" is found in:

a) Romans 3:23
b) Romans 4:23
c) Romans 5:23
d) Romans 6:23

## Question #7

John says the people who saw Jesus beheld His glory, which was full of:

a) God's love
b) God's Spirit
c) grace and truth
d) goodness and truth

## Question #8

Whose raising to life was said to show "the glory of God"?

a) Jairus' daughter
b) Eutychus
c) Dorcas
d) Lazarus

## Question #9

The last part of the Lord's Prayer says God's glory is:

a) forever
b) everlasting
c) eternal
d) unending

## Question #10

Psalm 24 says five times that God is the ___________ of glory.

a) Lord
b) King
c) Prince
d) Author

# GOD'S GLORY
## ANSWERS

1. c) heavens
2. d) all of the above
3. a) the ark of the covenant was taken (1 Samuel 4:17, 22)
4. b) had to leave (1 Kings 8:6, 10–11)
5. d) confess that Jesus Christ is Lord (Philippians 2:11)
6. a) Romans 3:23
7. c) grace and truth (John 1:14)
8. d) Lazarus (John 11:40–43)
9. a) forever (Matthew 6:13)
10. b) King (Psalm 24:7–10)

**So, how did you do?**

## MORE FUN BIBLE TRIVIA

*Quick Bible Quizzes* is a great way to pass time while polishing your memory of God's Word. These 300 quizzes, covering a wide range of topics, each contain five questions—long enough to engage your brain but short enough to finish before the deli calls your number!

Paperback / ISBN 978-1-63609-603-2